FIREFLIES

A HAUNTING TALE OF TRANSCENDING LOVE

K.D. PHILLIPS

Copyright © 2024 K.D. Phillips

All rights reserved. This book, or any portion thereof, may not be reproduced or used in any manner whatsoever without the express written permission of the publisher, except for the use of brief quotations in a book review. This is a work of fiction. Names, characters, businesses, places, events, and incidents are either the products of the author's imagination or used in a fictitious manner. Any resemblance to actual persons, living or dead, or actual events is purely coincidental.

No copyright infringement intended. No claims have been made over songs and/or lyrics written. All credit goes to the original owner.

Content Advisory: This book contains instances of strong language and depictions of violence. Reader discretion is advised.

Publication Design: Seven Fourteen Media, LLC

Cover Art: DLP@sevenfourteenmedia.net

"In the process of creating this book, we decided to contribute a portion of the proceeds to aid a charitable organization that crafts retreats for terminally and seriously ill children and their families. Amidst the tempest of illness, these sanctuaries offer respite, a haven where families can mend, connect, and rediscover the warmth of faith and friendship.

With the purchase of this book, you have become a silent companion to families facing unimaginable challenges. Let this book be more than a tale; may it be a conduit of love, extending its embrace to those in need."

K. D. Phillips

DEDICATION

If my people, who are called by my name, will humble themselves and pray and seek my face and turn from their wicked ways, then I will hear from heaven, and I will forgive their sin and will heal their land.

2 Chronicles 7:14

Contents

1. A Scene From a Postcard — 1
2. A Fleeting Shadow — 16
3. Time to Get Help — 32
4. Is This The Right Place? — 48
5. Spiders and Pizza — 67
6. This Ain't Yo Mama's Ghost Tour — 83
7. Lawrence Laine's Starlight Review — 99
8. Isn't It Strange? — 107
9. Shadows In the Trees — 125
10. The Cool Kat Club — 143
11. A Birthday Party — 157
12. The Letter — 169
13. Angel — 183
14. Do You Have Link Sausage? — 199
15. Time to Dig — 211
16. Let Your Demons Devour You — 226

17. "Bucket's Full"	243
18. Saying Goodbye	264
19. Fireflies	272
About the Author	285

Chapter One

A Scene From a Postcard

I slipped my sunglasses down the bridge of my nose and carefully steered between the other cars on the freeway. The sun was blinding, and I struggled to see through the haze of light even with tinted lenses. The traffic had thinned considerably since I left the city, leaving plenty of room for me to navigate. I carefully changed lanes, feeling the vibration in my hands as the tires rolled over the rumble strips. I felt my shoulders relax and let one hand wander from the steering wheel to lightly stroke my daughter Maddie's hair as she slept peacefully in the seat next to me. Her gentle breaths were rhythmic and reassuring in the quiet of the car.

My cell phone began to vibrate in the cup holder next to me, a jarring noise against the background silence. Careful not to wake Maddie, I retrieved the phone and let out a surprised gasp when I saw the name on the screen: Arthur Jameson, the Editor-in-Chief of the magazine I worked for.

"Hello?" I whispered, keeping my voice low.

"Is this Samantha Payne?" Arthur's deep voice was formal and authoritative. I tried to remember the last time we had spoken directly; it must have been shortly after I was hired several years ago.

"Uh, yes, this is Sam," I replied, doing my best to sound professional despite the whispered tone of my voice.

"Ah, Sam, I hope I'm not interrupting anything important." Arthur's voice was softer now, almost apologetic. "I just wanted to touch base with you personally."

"Of course, Mr. Jameson. I appreciate that... is there anything I can help you with?"

"Actually, Sam, it's more about what I might be able to help you with..."

As Arthur talked, I was struck by how much my life, and Maddie's, had changed in such a short amount of time. The past few months had been filled with doctors, treatments, consultations, and heartache.

"Sam, are you still there?" Arthur's voice pulled me back to the present, reminding me that I was still on the phone with one of the most powerful men in the publishing industry.

"Sorry, Mr. Jameson. Yes, I'm here. Thank you for thinking of us."

"Of course, Sam. We're all rooting for you and Maddie." His words were sincere and comforting, and I knew that they came from a place of genuine concern. "I can't tell you how sorry I am to hear about your leave of absence, but under these circumstances, I completely understand."

"Thank you, sir," I whispered, glancing over at Maddie, who remained peacefully asleep.

"May I ask... how Maddie is doing?" His question was

delicate, like he was trying to step carefully around broken glass.

I sighed, feeling the weight of Maddie's diagnosis pressing down on me. "She's okay... weak but good for now. She's asleep next to me."

There was a pause, and I could sense he was gathering his thoughts. "I want you to know that our prayers are with you both during this difficult time, and I hope you find some measure of comfort in the time you have left together."

"Thank you," I managed to choke out, feeling the tears prickling at the corners of my eyes.

"Several years ago, I lost my son," he confessed, his voice wavering slightly. "It was the hardest thing I've ever gone through. But I promise you, Sam – life does get better. It may not seem like it now, but it will."

"Mr. Jameson, your support means a lot to me. I hope to be writing again soon, once Maddie and I have had some time together." I couldn't keep the tremor from my voice, the emotions still raw.

"Take all the time you need, Samantha. We'll be here when you're ready," he said warmly.

"Thank you," I whispered, and with that, we ended the call.

I thought about the day the doctors delivered Maddie's diagnosis. I remembered the sterile smell of the hospital, the way my heart had hammered in my chest as they spoke of her rare blood disorder. At just seven years old, my little girl's life had changed forever.

"Bone marrow transplant," the doctor had said. "It's an

aggressive treatment, but it could be the key to saving her life." We attempted the procedure, but fate was cruel, and the transplant failed to slow the progress of this ruthless disease. Now, with only a few months left, I wanted to share my time with Maddie in a more peaceful place. We needed a break from the endless tumult of city life, a place where we could simply just be alone together.

I took a deep breath, shaking off the emotions that threatened to swallow me whole. I needed to focus on something else, anything to get out of this dreary funk. Turning my attention to the car's map display, I checked our progress. It had been just over two hours since we left the city, and with a little more than two hours remaining, we were making good time.

A part of me ached at the thought of leaving my work behind, of stepping away from the life I had built for myself. I knew that taking this leave of absence was my best choice, and I wanted to make the most of the time I had left with my little girl.

"Mama?" Maddie's soft voice pulled me from my thoughts.

"Hey there, sleepyhead," I murmured, my heart swelling with love. "Did you have a good nap?"

"Uh-huh," she replied, rubbing her eyes. "Are we almost there?"

"We still have a few hours to go, but we're making good time. We'll be there soon."

"Okay," Maddie sighed, snuggling back into her seat. She drifted back to sleep; her small hand wrapped around my finger.

FIREFLIES

The trees that flanked the freeway were a welcome change from the towering skyscrapers and throngs of people I'd become accustomed to having around me. The sight of the landscape was soothing, and I felt a sense of calm wash over me.

"Hang in there, Maddie," I silently urged, my heart aching with both love and despair. "We'll make the most of this new adventure, I promise."

I followed the signs leading us to Leesburg, Virginia, and turned off I-95 onto US-15. The small town seemed untouched by time, with old stone buildings standing as proud testaments to the past. Maddie and I bounced along in the car, marveling at the sights around us as we drove up Old Waterford Road. Trees lining the narrow lane cast a dappled shade across the rocky roadway, and fields dotted with wildflowers greeted us around every turn. Deer grazed peacefully as we drove past, completely unfazed by our presence. It all felt like a scene from a postcard, untouched and serene.

We continued our climb up the narrow road leading to the crest of a hill, encircled by thick trees that parted as we reached the top. I slowly eased the car through the open gate and into the yard outside the old farmhouse.

"Are we here? Is this it?" Maddie eyes shined with excitement.

"Looks like it! What do you think?" I studied her face

intently, hoping to read her thoughts.

"It has barns!" she screamed as she threw open the car door and ran for a closer look. "Can we go inside them?"

"Yeah, in a little while, but first, let's get moved in."

The farmhouse sat proudly on three and a half acres of land, with the road that led to the old village of Waterford forming a natural boundary at the front. An old wooden fence surrounded the property, with broken boards leaving gaps like missing teeth in many places. The once-vibrant white paint had peeled away, revealing the rough texture of the wood beneath. Even in its weathered state, there was something undeniably charming about it.

A dirt road snaked its way up from the main road to a side entrance, leading to a small part of the house that looked like it had been added long after the original structure was built. It gave it an almost haphazard appearance, as if it had grown organically over time, shaped by the needs and desires of those who had called it home.

"Mama, look at these!" Maddie yelled, holding out a small bouquet of delicate purple blossoms.

"Very pretty," I replied, smiling at her enthusiasm. "Let's take 'em inside and find a place for them, maybe in your new room?"

"Yes!" she screamed, scampering back toward the house.

With a gentle twist, the key turned in the old lock and I pushed open the door. A musty smell stung my nostrils as I stepped inside. Empty bookcases framed an impressive stone wall that stretched across one side of the room. A majestic fireplace opened in the center, its brickwork contrasting with the stone around it. It was illuminated by the late afternoon sunlight streaming through a large plate glass window on the opposite wall. Dusty sheets covered every piece of furniture, giving them a ghostly appearance. Everything about the farmhouse screamed history, and I loved it.

"Mama, do you think there's ghosts hiding in here?" Maddie asked, looking at the covered furnishings.

"Maybe," I chuckled. "If so, I'm sure they'll be friendly."

Maddie raced through the living room, skidded into the kitchen and out of sight. I listened as her feet made their way up stairs, then heard her running on the floor above. Within moments she reappeared.

"I found my room... come look!" Maddie shrieked as she reached out and grabbed my hand.

"Okay, show me," I said with a smile, allowing Maddie to pull me through the dimly lit rooms.

I took in the details of each room as we made our way through the house. The wallpaper was slightly faded, but still held its intricate floral design. The floorboards creaked beneath our feet as Maddie guided me up a narrow flight of stairs that led from the kitchen.

"Here it is!" Maddie announced, spinning with her arms out as she ran into the bedroom. Sunlight streamed through the rippled glass windows, casting a warm glow over the entire room. An antique four-poster bed sat against one wall, adorned with a patchwork quilt that looked as if it had been lovingly stitched together by someone's grandmother. Maddie's flowers had been gently placed on the quilt.

"Wow, Maddie, this is beautiful," I breathed, genuinely

impressed by how well the room suited my little girl. "Do you like it?"

"I love it," Maddie replied, her eyes shining with happiness. "It feels like...like I'm supposed to be here."

"Then let's make this your special place," I said, ruffling her hair affectionately. "We can put up some pictures and maybe find a nice rug for the floor."

"Can we put up fairy lights too?" Maddie asked, her eyes pleading. "I want it to be magical."

"We can do that. We'll make this room as magical as you can imagine."

"Promise?"

"Promise."

"Let's explore the rest of the house!" Maddie's energy seemingly endless despite her weakened state.

"We'll do a walk-thru, but then it's time for some rest, okay?" I didn't want to dampen her excitement.

"Okay," Maddie agreed, before dashing off down the narrow stairs, her laughter echoing through the rooms below.

As we continued to explore, I couldn't help but feel that the place was embracing us, welcoming us into its fold like long-lost family. The living room, with its worn leather armchairs and stone fireplace, seemed to beckon us to curl up with a good book on a cold winter's night. The quaint kitchen, with its wooden cupboards and checkered curtains, whispered of warm meals to be cooked and shared.

I looked out the window at the fireflies, beginning to emerge like tiny stars in the twilight. In that moment, I knew... we were exactly where we were meant to be.

→→ ·•· ←←

Maddie's laughter echoed in my mind as I pulled delicate dresses and toys from their cardboard confines. Each box I unpacked made our new life here feel more real, yet the question hung heavy in my mind: why had such a beautiful home been left empty for so long? I paused, leaning against the window frame to take in the breathtaking view of rolling hills and trees surrounding the property. The vibrant shades of green seemed to stretch on forever, like a lush embrace from Mother Nature herself.

Maddie's voice pulled me from my reverie. "What Cha doing?"

"Unpacking your things," I replied, smiling down at her standing at the bottom of the stairs. "You can come help me if you want."

Her footsteps beat on the worn wooden steps, each one creaking slightly under her weight.

"Remember this?" I asked, holding up a dress adorned with flowers. "You looked so pretty with it on."

"I did, didn't I," she replied, reaching out to touch the fabric. "It's pretty like this place... I like it here." Maddie giggled excitedly as she turned and ran back downstairs.

"Me too," I yelled after her, feeling a surge of hope and love fill my heart. Within minutes I could hear muffled voices from the television playing in the family room below. I picked up the empty box and made my way down the narrow staircase. Each step sloped gently towards the middle, polished smooth by the countless trips of others.

I moved through the kitchen to the back door, stepping out onto the small porch where I set the empty box next to others. My gaze fell upon the metal storm doors nearby that led to the cellar below. There was something intriguing about the unexplored spaces of this old house. It seemed like there were secrets everywhere just waiting to be revealed. I vowed to explore the cellar when I had more time. I stepped back into the kitchen, breathing in the smell of aged wood and coffee.

"Hey, Maddie," I called out as I opened another box. "Are you watching TV?"

"Uh-huh," came her distracted reply.

I walked through the old entry way that led to the newer addition of the farmhouse. As I entered the family room, I saw Maddie sitting only a few feet from the television, her small body wrapped in a blanket. An old black-and-white television show from the 1950s filled the screen, and I paused for a moment to watch.

"What's this?" I asked, taking a seat behind her on the worn sofa.

"An old show," she replied, her eyes never leaving the screen.

"Looks interesting," I commented, observing the grainy images of women in elegant dresses and men in sharp suits as they danced across the screen.

"It's fun to watch."

"It looks like it would be," I agreed, smiling. "But we need to finish setting things up, sweetie."

"I know," she moaned, tearing her eyes away from the screen with some effort. "Do we have to do it now?"

"Tell you what," I proposed, "You help me with these last boxes, and then we'll watch the rest of the show together... deal?"

"Deal," Maddie agreed, her face lighting up with a smile.

We returned to the kitchen and began unpacking. The last boxes were full of cans, spices and cooking utensils that Maddie placed in the cupboards with my direction. She seemed so determined to make sure that everything was just right, and I couldn't help but smile.

"Was that the last box?" Maddie looked around the room, hoping it was.

"Yep... last one."

"Good... so we can finish watching the show now?"

"If you want," I replied.

We held hands as we made our way back to the family room. The show Maddie had been watching was over, and a new one was starting, as if a series of reruns were being aired back-to-back.

"Wow, this is quite the show," I murmured as the glittering stage on the TV screen caught my attention. The camera panned over the audience, their faces full of excitement and anticipation. Maddie's eyes sparkled with fascination as she watched the vintage black-and-white program. I couldn't help but be drawn in by the atmosphere of the "*Starlight Revue*" and the captivating presence of its host, Lawrence Laine.

"I like him," Maddie stated boldly. Her gaze never left the screen as the tall, dark-haired man took center stage. His confidence was infectious, and I found myself smiling at his charismatic charm.

"Good evening, ladies and gentlemen!" Lawrence greeted the audience, his voice rich and warm. "Tonight, we have a spectacular lineup of talented performers for your enjoyment, from breathtaking dancers to uproarious comedians!"

Maddie jumped up from the floor and joined me on the couch, leaning against my side. I wrapped an arm around her, pulling her close as we watched the enchanting spectacle unfold before us.

"Did you know," Maddie said suddenly, her voice filled with excitement, "did you know that he used to live near here?"

"Lawrence Laine? Really?" I asked, feeling somewhat confused. "How do you know that?"

"I just know," she replied with a certainty that surprised me.

"Lawrence Laine, huh?" I echoed; my curiosity aroused. "Well, that's certainly... interesting."

I stood and walked over to the television to turn it off, much to Maddie's dismay. I shrugged and looked at her, hoping to dispel the feeling of bewilderment that had settled over me.

"Come on, sweetheart," I said, offering her a gentle smile. "Let's go sit on the front porch for a while."

"Okay," Maddie agreed, her voice soft and accepting. I hurried to grab the blanket off the floor before leading her out the front door.

The sun had dipped below the horizon, leaving streaks

of pink and orange in its wake. A cool breeze rustled the leaves of the towering oaks that surrounded our new home, their branches outstretched like ancient guardians.

"Isn't it beautiful out here?" I asked as we settled into a pair of rocking chairs on the porch. Maddie nodded, snuggling beneath the blanket I had draped around her.

"Look, the fireflies are dancing," she whispered, pointing to the twinkling lights that floated just above the grass. I watched as they weaved intricate patterns in the air, their tiny bodies glowing with an otherworldly glow. Maddie leaned against me, her breathing slow and labored. She didn't speak again for a while, her gaze fixed on the fireflies that had begun to dance in the twilight.

"Fireflies are actually little insects that produce a glow in their bellies," I explained to Maddie, her eyes wide with fascination. "Some people think they're special messengers, like little spirits, or the souls of people who have passed away."

"I know they're spirits."

I could sense that Maddie's conviction came from judgements formed in deep thought.

"Why do you think that?" I asked gently.

"I just... know it."

"Like you knew the man on the TV show used to live near here?" I couldn't help but ask, remembering her earlier statement.

"Yep... just like that," she nodded, her voice filled with certainty.

We sat there for a while in the fading light, watching the shadows spread across the valley below us. Eventually,

I decided it was time for dinner, so I fetched a couple of sandwiches from the kitchen. We ate together, our laughter mingling with the songs of crickets and the rustle of leaves in the wind. My turkey sandwich had never tasted so good, as if the simple act of sharing a meal on this porch filled each bite with an extra layer of flavor.

As the night deepened and the stars began to emerge overhead, Maddie grew tired. Her once-vibrant eyes started to droop, and her laughter faded into soft sighs.

"Time for bed," I said softly, brushing a stray curl from her forehead.

"Okay," she agreed with a yawn as she gazed out into the night one last time.

"Mama, I don't want to be sick anymore," she whispered, her voice trembling. "I want to stay here with you forever."

My heart ached at her words, and I fought back tears as I hugged her closer. "I know, baby," I whispered into her hair. "I wish I could make it all go away."

I held onto that moment, the stillness of the air and the gentle rhythm of Maddie's breathing, knowing that these memories would be my lifeline in the days to come. Gently, I scooped Maddie's frail body into my arms, her warmth seeping into my chest as I carried her up the creaking stairs.

"Mama," Maddie mumbled sleepily, her eyes fluttering open. "Will you sing me the ponies song?"

"Of course, baby," I whispered, tenderly laying her down on the crisp white sheets in her new room. The window beside her bed framed a stunning view of the rolling hills outside, which seemed to stretch endlessly under the starlit sky. Tucking her in, I began to sing:

Close your eyes, my little one,
Let the dreams of ponies run,
Through the meadows, oh so bright,
While you sleep this starry night.

Maddie's eyelids grew heavier with each verse, her breaths deepening as she surrendered to slumber. I placed a gentle kiss on her forehead before I left her side, the tranquility of the moment etched in my heart.

Moving down the stairs, I walked through the dimly lit house. The moon offered its own source of light, casting long shadows on the walls and floors as I entered my bedroom and slipped between the cool sheets. I lay there in the quiet embrace of the old farmhouse and whispered a heartfelt prayer.

"Please... let us find peace here."

My words mingled with the rustle of leaves outside, carried away on the wind. As dreams began to weave their magic, I allowed myself to believe that miracles could indeed happen within these walls.

Chapter Two

A Fleeting Shadow

I stretched lazily beneath the covers, my body tingling with the warmth that seeped through the window. The first rays of sunlight poured into the room, bathing it in a soft, golden glow. The sound of birds filled the air, a symphony of trills and warbles that heralded the dawn of a new day.

"Good morning," I whispered to the empty room, inhaling the sweet scent of dew-kissed blossoms that wafted in through the open window. With a sigh, I swung my legs over the side of the bed, grabbed my robe and slipped into my slippers, my thoughts turning to the day ahead.

I walked into the kitchen and reached for the coffee pot, setting it on the stove. The gentle hiss of the gas burner coming to life broke the silence, and I grabbed my phone from the counter. My thumb moved instinctively to unlock the screen, and I scanned my inbox for any emails. There was one text message, a simple note from my managing editor: "I'll call you later... might have you work on something."

"Interesting," I mumbled as I tucked the phone into the pocket. The rich aroma of coffee enveloped me, comforting and familiar, as I poured myself a cup and took a slow, appreciative sip.

"Better check on Maddie." I thought, setting my coffee down as I crept up the stairs. I paused at the top, listening for any sign of movement. It seemed peacefully quiet, with only the slight rustle of bedsheets hinting that Maddie was stirring.

"You up?" I asked gently, noticing her eyes fluttering open in the dim light.

"I'm getting there," Maddie replied with a thick, sleepy voice.

"Brush your teeth and throw on some clothes when you get a little more awake. I'll make breakfast."

"Okay," Maddie mumbled, rubbing her eyes as she sat up in bed.

Descending the stairs, my thoughts turned to the message from work. I wondered why there might be some work for me since I'd just been granted a leave of absence to be with Maddie.

The kitchen hummed with activity as I began to prepare breakfast, the sizzle of bacon and the crackle of eggs frying filled the air. My phone buzzed on the counter... probably my editor. I took a deep breath and answered the call.

"This is Sam."

"Sam, it's Janice," my editor began, her tone warm yet professional. "I had a thought and wanted to run it by you. I think it might be good for you to write something while you're there... you know, a little article to help keep your mind off things... but it's totally up to you."

"I suppose I could write something as long as Maddie is feeling ok."

"Not mandatory," she replied. "I know you need to focus on her so it would just be in your spare time. It was just a thought... just wanting to help you get your mind on something positive."

"Alright," I agreed hesitantly. "But I'd like to write something that allows me to continue looking into possible treatments for Maddie. Maybe there's an interesting local connection I can look into."

"That would work," Janice agreed without hesitation. "I'll leave the subject matter up to you."

"Thanks for thinking about me, Janice," I breathed, feeling a hint of relief. "I'll see what I can come up with."

"Keep me posted on everything," she said warmly and ended the call. "That was nice of Janice to offer me a distraction," I thought. "She knew I needed one."

Taking a sip of my coffee, I called out for Maddie, "You ready for breakfast?"

There was no response.

"Maddie, honey, I've got your food ready... don't let it get cold."

Silence was my only reply.

An uneasy feeling settled in my stomach as I made my way up the narrow staircase.

"Sweetheart?" I called out, trying to mask my fear. I hesitated at the threshold of Maddie's room, feeling a bone-chilling cold unlike anything I'd ever felt before.

"Maddie?" I whispered softly, my breath visible in the

cold air.

There was no response, no familiar laughter or playful banter to fill the silence. Maddie's bed looked curiously untouched, neatly made up as if it had never been slept in. My chest tightened... my motherly instincts on high alert as I tried to make sense of it all.

"Maddie?" I called again, my voice quivering with urgency. I turned toward the adjacent bathroom, thinking I would find her there. The cold intensified as I moved closer, a frigid chill that seemed to gnaw at my soul. Dread coiled within me, tightening like a vice around my heart, yet I forced myself to continue.

"Please be okay," I muttered under my breath, worried that Maddie's illness had taken her from me.

The quaint bathroom embraced me as I stepped inside, my gaze lingering on the vintage tiles beneath my feet. Each one seemed to tell a tale of decades long past, their faded beauty a testament to the history that had unfolded within these walls.

My eyes were drawn to the large, ornate mirror dominating the room. An image stared back at me from its slightly fogged surface, and I was startled to realize that it was my own reflection. My eyes betrayed a mixture of anxiety and tiredness... a mother lost in her own fears, searching for answers. I swallowed hard, fighting back emotion.

"Come on, Maddie," I muttered under my breath, revealing my frustration. "This isn't funny. Where are you hiding?"

As if in response, there it was—a flicker of movement,

a fleeting shadow that darted across the mirror's surface. My breath hitched, my heart skipping a beat as disbelief warred with the undeniable truth before me.

In the mirror, a young girl appeared—pale, ethereal, and transient. Her hair, dark as midnight, cascaded in loose waves down her back, the strands seemingly defying the laws of gravity. Her eyes, large and hauntingly deep, held a timeless wisdom that belied her youthful face.

My heart pounded in my chest, echoing the wild drumbeat of fear and awe that coursed through me. The girl moved with a grace I had never witnessed before, her lithe form dancing effortlessly through the cramped space. I held my breath, watching her every movement. Tension knotted within me, a tightly wound spring just waiting to snap. An airy gasp escaped my lips as it dawned on me—this little girl was not my Maddie.

"Who are you?" I breathed, my voice barely there. "Are you... real?"

The girl said nothing, but her gaze seemed to bore into my soul, as if she could see every hope and fear that lay hidden within my heart.

"Please," I whispered desperately, my eyes brimming with tears. "If you know anything about Maddie, tell me. I need to find her."

In that moment, our gazes locked, and I felt an inexplicable connection to this spectral figure. It was as though we shared the same heartbeat, our lives intertwined by some unseen force.

"Are you here to help Maddie?" I pressed, desperation giving strength to my voice. Still, the girl remained silent.

FIREFLIES

My heart ached with the need to understand, to find some semblance of meaning in this spiritual encounter. The girl's gaze never wavered, and for a moment, I thought I saw a flicker of compassion in her eyes. As quickly as she had appeared, she began to fade, her ethereal form dissolving like mist beneath the first rays of dawn.

"Wait!" I cried out, my hand reaching out instinctively to touch the mirror's cold surface, but it was too late. The girl had vanished, leaving behind only a lingering sense of loss and the echo of a whispered word:

"Believe."

"Believe," I repeated quietly. My heart ached with the weight of love, despair, and hope—a complex tapestry of emotions that threatened to overwhelm me. As I stood there, surrounded by the remnants of an encounter that seemed to defy all logic, I made a silent promise to myself: for Maddie, I would believe in anything. Even the impossible.

"Mama?" Maddie's voice called out hesitantly from the next room, causing me to jump. I turned to see her laying in her bed clutching a stuffed animal tightly to her chest.

"Maddie?" I gasped, very confused. "I was just... I didn't see you there when I came up."

"Is everything okay?" Maddie asked as she sat up in the tangle of blankets surrounding her.

"Of course...stay right there," I assured her, forcing a smile. Returning to Maddie's side, I perched myself on the edge of her bed, fighting to keep my composure. "Did you just get back in bed?" I asked, hoping that the strange vision I'd recently witnessed had a simple explanation.

"I just rolled over and saw you standing in the bathroom." she replied with a puzzled look.

"Did you see anyone else in the room with me?" I questioned, my eyes searching her face for any sign of understanding.

"Uh-huh." she nodded, her voice still thick with sleep. "I saw my new friend with you. She's nice, isn't she. I met her in my dreams."

"You met her in your dreams?" I asked, my throat clenched with a mix of fear and curiosity.

"She's my age," Maddie continued, a smile spreading across her lips. "She made me laugh and told me stories. I think she used to live in this house... in this room."

A cold feeling seeped into my bones, chilling me to my core, but I couldn't let Maddie see my fear. Holding back my need for more answers, I simply said, "Sounds like you had fun."

My eyes scanned the room for any sign of the mysterious girl as I helped Maddie dress. Everything seemed normal, with the sun's rays peeking through the sheer curtains, and a subtle hint of lavender wafting in the air.

"Come on," I whispered, taking Maddie by the hand. "Let's get some breakfast." I took her hand, guiding her down the creaky staircase and into the kitchen.

"Mama," Maddie said softly, breaking the silence as she climbed onto a chair at the kitchen table. "Do you believe in ghosts?"

I hesitated for a moment, weighing my words carefully. "I believe that there are things in this world we don't fully understand." I replied. "Maybe we're not supposed to understand... maybe we just accept and move on."

⇉ ·•◆•· ⇇

We drove along the winding country road leading to Waterford, admiring the picturesque landscape as it rolled past. It was a short drive from the farmhouse, and we arrived quickly, parking near the Corner Store on Main Street. Its charming exterior beckoned us inside with its colorful awnings and hand-painted sign. A bell above the door jingled merrily as we entered, announcing our arrival. Shelves upon shelves of knickknacks and trinkets filled every available space. A sense of nostalgia washed over me, harkening back to simpler times when magic still lingered in the corners of my imagination.

"Mama, can I have this?" Maddie asked, her wide eyes fixed on a hand-sewn doll displayed prominently on a nearby shelf. The doll's delicate features were brought to life with painstaking detail, her porcelain skin and rosy cheeks hinting at the love and care that had been poured into her creation. She wore a beautiful, lace-trimmed dress, her golden hair cascading over her shoulders like a waterfall of sunlight. As Maddie cradled the doll in her arms, a small smile tugged at the corners of her mouth.

"Can I have her, please?" she asked softly, her eyes pleading.

"I guess so," I replied, unable to resist her hopeful expression.

Maddie hugged the doll close and whispered, "I'm going

to name you Amelia."

"Amelia?" I felt a sense of unease as I repeated the name, but brushed it aside, focusing instead on the joy radiating from Maddie's face.

"Excuse me," I said, turning to the store attendant behind the counter. "I'm thinking of writing an article about this area and I think the Corner Store would be a perfect feature. Do you have any information or interesting stories you could share?"

"Sure," the attendant replied warmly, launching into a fascinating history of the store and its significance to the community.

I scribbled a few words in my notebook as we talked. During a lull in the conversation my gaze fell upon a poster displayed in the store window. It advertised a monthly ghost tour in nearby Leesburg. The thought of delving into the town's supernatural side intrigued me, especially considering our morning's events.

"Do you know anything about this ghost tour?" I asked the attendant, pointing to the poster.

"Oh, that's a fun," she said with a knowing smile. "It's quite popular with tourists, but lots of the local ladies attend as well."

"Really? Why's that?"

"Well," she leaned in conspiratorially, "the women around here seem especially fond of the tour guide, if you catch my drift." I couldn't help but chuckle at her subtle insinuation. "He's a really good-looking paranormal investigator who, I've been told, casts quite a spell!"

The thought of meeting someone who could maybe

explain the weird events happening at our place intrigued me, and I wrote down the flyer's number. "Worth checking into," I thought, "and if this guy is as handsome as they claim...that wouldn't be a bad thing." I felt my cheeks flush, and I couldn't help but smile. "Believe," I whispered softly to myself.

"What was that, dear?" the attendant asked with a puzzled look.

"Oh... sorry... just thinking out loud... thanks for your help," I answered, as I grabbed Maddie's hand and quickly walked out of the store.

"Believe," I whispered once more as we walked to the car. Maddie's new doll Amelia was nestled securely in her arms. "I could use some of that," I thought, envying Maddie's loving embrace of a new best friend.

⋙ ⋅✦⋅ ⋘

We returned home, laden with bags from the afternoon shopping spree. Maddie talked endlessly with her new doll, Amelia, sharing everything that came to mind about her life. Amelia just smiled; a frozen painted-on grin that made her seem happy to be part of the family.

"Can we put Amelia on my bed?"

"I think that's a great idea." I replied, smiling affectionately.

We spent the rest of the afternoon and evening relaxing and talking about our day. Just spending time together brought a sense of comfort that I hadn't realized I'd been craving. After dinner, I tucked Maddie into bed, kissing her forehead as I whispered goodnight. She snuggled up to Amelia as she drifted off to sleep.

I withdrew downstairs to my makeshift office, determined to write a bit for Janice. I settled in at the kitchen table, my laptop clicking under my fingers as I began to type. My mind wandered... from the Corner Store to the ghost tour, and then to the handsome paranormal investigator mentioned by the store attendant.

"Could he possibly help me figure out what happened this morning with that ghost girl? I mean, he is into that kinda stuff."

My train of thought derailed as the faint sound of footsteps and laughter floated down from above. Anxiety ran through me as I hurriedly climbed the stairs to Maddie's room, only to find her peacefully asleep, her new doll nestled securely in her arms. Confused but reassured, I turned to walk back downstairs.

As I descended into the kitchen, a palpable shift in temperature stopped me in my tracks. That same cold sensation I experienced earlier had returned, wrapping itself around me like a blanket.

Fear and disbelief ran through me as I stared at the strange display before me. Every cupboard door in the kitchen stood open; a surreal picture that defied logic and reason. Plates and bowls peeked out from the half-opened doors, a silent testament to the inexplicable.

"Wh-what the...?" I stammered; my breath caught in my throat. My heart raced, but a small smile tugged at the corner of my lips. This was all so absurd yet terrifying at the same time. I couldn't just run away; Maddie was asleep upstairs. I willed myself to walk into the kitchen, the cold air stinging my skin. I rubbed the chill from my arms as I went around closing each cupboard door. The room seemed to grow warmer with each click of a door snapping shut.

"That wasn't so bad," I whispered to myself, trying to ease the lingering fear. "Guess I won't be writing anything tonight." I mumbled as I shut down my laptop and turned off the lights, plunging the room into darkness. Each step into the entryway and towards my bedroom felt like an eternity, the floorboards creaking beneath my feet.

I stopped in my tracks as I noticed eerie shapes dancing across the walls of the corridor, flickering like hungry flames. They seemed to have no source of light for their creation, and I studied them for a moment, frozen in place. "There's got to be a logical explanation for this," I thought, but my unease won control over rational thinking. I abandoned the idea of sleeping in my own room and headed for Maddie's instead. The moment I slid into Maddie's bed, her warm presence offered me a sense of safety. It felt like a shield against the strange events plaguing our home.

"Get your shit together, Sam," I scolded myself, feeling foolish for letting fear get the best of me. No matter how hard I tried, I couldn't relax. Every noise outside and inside the house kept me awake and on edge. After what seemed like hours, exhaustion finally claimed me, and I drifted off into a restless sleep.

The sound of the television coming to life in the family

room jolted me awake.

"Oh hell no." I thought, my blood running cold. Bolting from the bed I raced down the stairs, my heart hammering in my chest.

The television bathed the room in an eerie glow. Reflections paraded on the walls like sinister imps. An old black-and-white program filled the screen: "*Lawrence Laine's Starlight Revue.*"

"This isn't a coincidence," I thought with a shiver, realizing that whatever ghostly presence was haunting this house was trying to communicate something important. But what could it be? What did it want us to know?

Tearing my gaze away from the flickering images on the screen, I reached to switch off the old TV, pausing just as my fingers brushed against the knob. An unsettling feeling crept over me, and I knew that turning off the television wouldn't bring an end to this bizarre event.

"Help me understand," I whispered, my voice trembling. "What are you trying to tell me? What do you want?"

The room filled with music, a thin, shrill song that echoed from the set. I stood there watching, waiting for a sign... anything that would help me make sense of this nightmare. My pulse quickened as a young woman began to sing, her voice hauntingly beautiful.

> *In shadows deep, I took my flight,*
> *Lost in the veil of endless night.*
> *A child once, with dreams so bright,*
> *Now a whisper, a ghostly sight.*

I gasped as I listened to the words. The singer's image faded in-and-out, but the music and lyrics remained strong.

> *A mother's love, a daughter's grace,*
> *The answers lie in time and space.*
> *Healing waits in truth's embrace,*
> *For in understanding, we find our place.*

The song ended and the singer bowed gracefully as cheers filled the air. I couldn't shake the feeling that this song was somehow connected to the little girl I had seen in the mirror.

"Please," I murmured in a quiet voice, "don't hurt my daughter."

I knew that whatever force haunted our home had taken an interest in Maddie, and the thought terrified me more than anything I could imagine. My love for her was my greatest strength and my deepest vulnerability. All I could do was pray that I could somehow protect her. I reached out and turned off the television, plunging the room into darkness.

As the screen went black, I heard the unmistakable sound of children laughing. My blood ran cold, and my thoughts immediately turned to Maddie. Panicked, I raced through the house and up the stairs, praying with each step that she was safe. I burst into her room, my eyes searching frantically in the dark... but Maddie wasn't there. Her bed was empty, the sheets strewn about as if she had left in a hurry.

"God, no," I choked out in a panicked cry as tears filled my eyes. A glowing light filled the window beside Maddie's bed, and I moved closer to look outside. Fireflies circled over the dew-covered grass, and in their midst, I saw two little girls holding hands and dancing... laughing as if they didn't have a care in the world.

"Maddie!" I yelled, pounding my fists against the glass. Fear quickly turned to fury as I dashed down the stairs and out the front door. I sprinted across the porch and into the yard, determined to reach her.

"Get away from her!" I screamed, my voice raw with terror.

In an instant, one girl vanished, like a wisp of smoke on the wind. I reached Maddie and pulled her into my arms, holding her tightly as I fought back sobs.

"Never, Maddie... you are never to leave the house at night unless I'm with you. Do you understand me?" My voice was trembling but stern.

"But Amelia wanted to show me the fireflies," Maddie protested, her innocent eyes betraying her confusion. "She said it was ok."

"Amelia? Your doll?"

"Not the doll!" Maddie sighed with exasperation. "My friend Amelia... you saw her this morning."

I scooped Maddie into my arms; her body felt so small and fragile against mine. I couldn't shake the overwhelming feeling that we were being watched as we made our way back to the house. Fireflies circled around us as I stepped onto the porch. A young girl's crying cut through the stillness of the night, growing in intensity as it echoed around the farmhouse like a chilling symphony.

"Mommy, what's that sound?" Maddie whispered, her small hands gripping my shirt tightly.

"Nothing, baby. Just the wind," I lied, trying to keep my voice steady. The truth was, I didn't know who or what it was, and that terrified me more than anything else.

"I'm scared." Maddie moaned, her tears wet against my shoulder.

"Shh, it's okay," I murmured, trying to reassure her even as fear gnawed at my own heart. "Everything's okay. I promise."

Fireflies swirled around the house, their glow casting eerie patterns on the walls. The air hummed with an unsettling energy, one that I could no longer ignore or pretend didn't exist. I didn't know who or what Amelia was, but it was clear that she wasn't just a figment of our imaginations. For Maddie's sake, I needed to get to the bottom of this, no matter how terrifying the truth may be... and that meant seeking help from someone who understood the paranormal world.

"Whatever you are," I whispered into the night, "you will not harm my child."

Chapter Three

Time to Get Help

The first rays of morning light filtered through the curtains as I stirred awake. I had spent the night curled up in the family room, leaning against an old leather chair where Maddie was peacefully sleeping. Glancing at the side door, I remembered why I had chosen this spot. With the car parked just outside, we could make a quick escape if necessary. The small fire I had lit in the fireplace had gone out, leaving behind smoking embers and a chilly draft. I sighed, recalling unplugging the TV to avoid being startled awake by any more old reruns.

"Morning already?" I sarcastically mumbled to myself, rubbing the sleep from my eyes, and stretching my limbs. The tension from last night seemed to have faded with the light of day, and I felt foolish for letting my imagination run wild. Still, I couldn't shake that feeling of needing help, even if it turned out to be nothing more than an overactive mind.

I looked out the large plate glass window, taking in the tranquil scene. Early morning light painted the valley below the farmhouse in soft hues, creating a sense of calm.

My gaze turned to the grass just outside the window, where trampled patterns revealed our footsteps from last night. I frowned, realizing that my optimism might need to be checked.

"Mama?" Maddie's sleepy voice broke my train of thought. "Is everything okay?"

"Everything's fine, sweetheart," I reassured her, forcing a smile. "Just looking outside."

"I'm still sleepy." she said, yawning.

"Why don't you stay here while I make some coffee, okay?"

"Okay," she replied, snuggling back into the chair.

As I walked into the kitchen, I couldn't help but feel a bit timid, wondering if there was any room in this house that hadn't displayed some form of paranormal activity. "Haunted house," I muttered under my breath with a nervous chuckle, trying to convince myself that it was all just a joke. After all, every old place is haunted, right?

I busied myself with brewing a fresh pot of coffee, the familiar aroma filling the air and helping to ease my lingering concern. I poured myself a steaming cup and sat down at the table. Opening my laptop, I began to review my notes from the interview I'd conducted at the Old Corner Store.

My eyes scanned the page, landing on the phone number I'd scribbled down for the Leesburg Ghost Tour. I felt a chill run through me as I recalled the strange events that had played out yesterday and last night. Real or imaginary, I wanted to talk to someone... anyone older than a child, who might be able to shed some light on what was going on.

"Why not?" I muttered to myself, reaching for my cell. "Nothing to lose." My heart raced as I dialed the number. Almost instantly, there was an answer, and I heard a recorded message filled with spooky screams, creaks, groans, and howling winds. I shook my head at the irony of it all as the message began:

"Oh, great, another moron calling about the Leesburg monthly ghost tour."

You could hear paper shuffling as the female voice continued speaking, clearly off-microphone, to someone else in the room.

"Like, seriously, do I have to read this?"

"Kat..." a male voice admonished her from the background.

"Fine, whatever." Her voice became clearer as she spoke directly into the mic.

"You've reached the Leesburg Ghost Escapades, where we'll take you on a tour that's probably not as scary as my mood right now."

"Stick to the script, Kat," the annoyed background voice interjected.

I rolled my eyes at the unprofessional recording but continued to listen. Despite the sarcasm dripping from the woman's voice, I couldn't help but hope someone might be able to provide insight into my situation.

"Yeah, yeah, I'm getting to it," she continued with a heavy sigh, clearly frustrated.

"Attention, fellow victims... uh, I mean, valued customers! The moon's out, the spirits are restless, and

FIREFLIES

we're bracing ourselves for another round of ghostly shenanigans. So, ready yourselves, because there's a tour tonight. Yep, you heard me. Tonight! The ghosts are getting ready to put on their best show, and by best, I mean they'll be trying to remember how to make things go bump in the night."

"Just finish it, please," the male voice whispered.

"Leave your name and number after the beep, and we'll add you to the list of people who willingly signed up for this ghostly rollercoaster." Her voice trailed off as she addressed her companion.

"Happy now?"

"That was amazing." the male voice muttered sarcastically.

"You know what, Normie?" Kat replied, "If you think you can do better, why don't you record the message?" She paused before mumbling under her breath.

"Jerk."

"I heard that, Kat."

The back-and-forth went on, both talking over one another until their exchange was abruptly cut off by the beep.

"Uh, hi," I hesitated, unsure how to respond to the odd recording. "My name is Samantha Payne, and I'm not interested in your tour, but I need help with a... ghost problem. If anyone there knows anything about real spirit encounters, please call me back at this number."

I hung up the phone, shaking my head at the strange recording.

"Who was that?" Maddie asked, her voice soft and groggy

as she entered the kitchen, still clutching her new doll.

"Nobody important," I replied, forcing a smile to reassure her. "Just left a message for someone who might be able to help us with our... well, you know."

"Amelia?" Maddie whispered, looking down at her doll as if sharing a secret.

"Right," I nodded, trying not to let my concern show. "Last night was... interesting, huh?"

"Amelia says you shouldn't be worried," Maddie replied, stretching her little arms up towards the ceiling. "She says ghosts aren't real."

"Not real?" I frowned, wondering where that comment came from. "Is she an expert?"

"Uh-huh," Maddie nodded, hugging her doll tightly. "She's really nice. She just likes to play tricks sometimes."

"Tricks, huh?" I mused, sipping my coffee as I pondered what that could mean. "Well, I left my cell number on the message. I'm hoping someone will get back to me soon so I can figure out Amelia and her tricks."

"Really?" Maddie's eyes widened with excitement. "Are they experts on tricks?"

"Um, something like that," I chuckled, smiling at her affectionately.

"I talked to her in my dreams last night."

"Her?" I asked cautiously, leaning forward in my chair. "You mean Amelia?"

"Uh-huh," Maddie nodded.

"Tell me about it," I urged gently, wanting to know more about the dream.

"Okay," she began, her little voice filled with enthusiasm.

"Amelia and I were playing together in a big field, and she was wearing a funny dress, like from a really long time ago. She told me that she didn't have any friends, just her mom, and she never got hugs from anyone."

"Really?"

"Yep," Maddie continued. "I told her that I would give her hugs whenever she wanted, and she was so happy! She even said that when I hug my doll, she can feel it too."

"Well, then I guess you'll have to give her lots of hugs, won't you?"

"Uh-huh!" Maddie agreed enthusiastically. "I'll give her all the hugs in the world!"

"So," I continued, trying to keep my voice light, "what else did you do in your dream?"

Maddie's eyes lit up. "She showed me her dollhouse... it was really cool! She said her mom wouldn't let her have any toys in the house, so she kept them all in the barn."

"You were in the barn in your dream?

"Yep. She has lots of toys in the barn so she took me there to show me."

"What kind of toys does she have?"

Maddie pursed her lips in thought, "there were lots of dolls against one wall... and there was this little table with a tea set and paper dolls with different outfits. Oh! And in the corner, there was a bookcase with games like Candy Land and Chutes and Ladders!"

"Wow," I marveled at the level of detail in Maddie's dream. "Anything else?"

Maddie nodded excitedly. "Amelia showed me a book she was reading, something about a witch. Can we get that book? I want to read it too."

"We don't know the title, Maddie, but if we figure it out, I'll get if for you," I agreed, though my head was spinning. How could Maddie have dreamt of such specific things?

"Mama, do you think Amelia is real?"

"I don't know, sweetheart," I admitted, stroking her hair. "But what matters is that she makes you happy, right?"

"Right!" Maddie agreed, hugging her doll tightly. "Can we go to the barn later and play with her toys?" Maddie eyes were wide with excitement.

I laughed, shaking my head. "Maddie, it was just a dream. I highly doubt there are any toys out there."

"But Mama..." she protested, looking disappointed.

"We'll see, okay?" I compromised, not wanting to completely crush her hopes. I sighed, trying to suppress the uneasy feeling I had about the old wooden barn out back. If Amelia was indeed a ghost, then exploring her domain seemed incredibly risky.

The shrill ring of my cell phone ended Maddie's complaints. I grabbed it and quickly answered.

"This is Sam."

"Hi, this is Chris Janney," a strong male voice replied. "I'm the lead paranormal investigator with the Leesburg Ghost Tours. You left a message earlier?"

"I did," I stammered, suddenly feeling foolish for making the call. "I didn't expect anyone to call back this quickly, to be honest. I just... well, I guess I've been experiencing some strange things here at our new house."

"Strange how?" Chris asked, his tone shifting from casual curiosity to professional interest.

FIREFLIES

I hesitated for a moment, taking in the normalcy of the sunlit room around me. "Well, my daughter Maddie and I just moved into a farmhouse on Old Waterford Road, and I think... I think something was already here."

"Ah, I see. New surroundings can often lead to feelings that there might be supernatural activity, especially in an older place like that," he replied skeptically. "It's probably nothing to worry about."

"Right, that's what I thought too," I agreed, feeling foolish for even bringing it up. "But do spirits often make themselves visible to those around them? Or is it more of a... I don't know, a feeling or something?"

"Rarely," Chris answered. "Most paranormal encounters involve sensing a presence, seeing shadows or balls of light – that sort of thing."

"I haven't seen any balls of light," I confessed, "Just a little girl."

"You've *seen* someone?" Chris sounded genuinely surprised. "Has your daughter seen her as well?"

"Yes," I admitted, bracing myself for more skepticism. "She even claims to have played with her." To my surprise, he seemed concerned rather than dismissive.

"Okay, this is definitely something we should discuss further. Would you be willing to come to our office with your daughter? We can go over your experiences with my team in more detail here."

"Sure," I agreed, grateful for his willingness to help. "When would be a good time?"

"Later this afternoon works for us," he said. "And if you're interested, we have a ghost tour tonight that you're welcome to join."

"Um, okay," I replied, intrigued by the idea. "That sounds interesting."

"Great, then I'll see you and your daughter later. Did you say her name was Maddie?"

"Yes, Maddie... she's eight. Is that too young for the tour?"

"Depends on if she'd be interested or not, but if she doesn't want to go, I can have one of my team members stay with her at the office. See you soon."

With that, he hung up, and I was left feeling a strange mix of relief and uncertainty. If there was even a slight chance that these encounters were real, then I owed it to Maddie, and to myself, to find out what was going on... and with Chris's help, maybe we could finally get some answers.

I made my way back into the family room where Maddie was standing by the window, gazing out at the barn.

"Can we go look for Amelia's toys now?"

"Sweetie... it was just a dream," I said gently, trying to dismiss her persistence, but there was something about the earnestness in her voice that tugged at my heart, making it hard to say no.

"Please, Mama?" she repeated, her gaze unwavering. "I really want to see if they're there."

"Alright," I finally relented, sighing. "Let's go take a look."

Maddie's face lit up, and together, we walked through the kitchen and out the back door. We descended the porch steps and crossed the dirt drive, and I felt a renewed sense of adventure. My concern about the barn seemed to dissipate in the warmth of the sun that embraced us.

"Come on, Mama!" Maddie urged, tugging at my hand. "Let's go see what's inside!"

"Okay, okay," I relented, allowing her to pull me forward. Maddie led me to a small door on one side, next to two larger ones that were bolted closed. We entered cautiously, the dim interior revealing a dusty, musty-smelling room that once housed feed and hay. Boxes were strewn about, and a large tarp covered a pile of things in one corner.

"Amelia toys are under that cloth," Maddie explained, pointing excitedly.

"Okay, let's take a look."

I hesitated for a moment, my heart racing as I reached for the dusty cloth. I couldn't help but feel a mix of anxiety and curiosity. What if Amelia was real? What if there really was a connection between this world and the spiritual one?

"Here goes nothing," I whispered, pulling the tarp aside.

The sight that greeted me was both eerie and fascinating. A collection of toys lay against the wall, identical to what Maddie had described in her dream. Rag dolls and baby dolls peered up at us with glassy eyes, while 'Candy Land' and 'Chutes and Ladders' sat atop a small bookcase nearby. Despite the layer of dust that clung to everything, it was clear that these items had once been cherished.

"See, Mama?" Maddie insisted, her eyes wide with wonder. "I told you they were here!"

"Sweetheart..." I began, the words catching in my throat. I didn't know what to say, how to reconcile the impossible truth before my eyes with everything I thought I knew about the world.

"Mama, look!" Maddie exclaimed, pointing to a book on

the table. "That's the book Amelia showed me!"

I picked up the well-worn novel, its cover depicting a young girl with a curious expression on her face. The title read *'The Mysterious Visitor by Kathryn Kenny - a Trixie Belden book.'* It seemed so ordinary, yet the fact that Maddie had seen it in her dream sent a chill through me.

I glanced around the dimly lit room, feeling an odd mixture of love, despair, and hope. Love for my daughter who had formed a connection with a ghost; despair at the thought that this little spirit girl had been trapped in our world without a family to care for her; and hope that perhaps, just maybe, we could do something to help her.

"Alright, Maddie," I said softly, placing the book back on the table. "You were right... the toys are here."

―――◆―――

The office above the bustling café in downtown Leesburg was a small cluttered one-room space that perfectly mirrored the eclectic personalities of its occupants. The room smelled of old books and coffee - a lingering aroma that traveled up from the eatery below. Chris Janney, the seasoned paranormal investigator in his late thirties, sat behind his cluttered desk, surveying his team members, engaged in their usual banter. Diplomas from pseudo-scientific institutions such as the 'Rhinoceros Institute for Parapsychological Research' and the 'Institute of Noetic Sciences' adorned the walls behind him, bearing witness to his years of training.

Norman Pete, or "Normie" – as he was affectionately known, had his nose buried in a thick tome about spectral phenomena. His lanky frame hunched over; he occasionally punctuated his reading with muttered exclamations. Surrounding him were various paranormal investigation tools such as infrared thermometers, Electromagnetic Field Meters, and Spirit Boxes... it seemed like he was part of the clutter himself. He wore a black t-shirt with white letters that read: "Fishing for Ghosts. Catch and Release Only," and above his desk hung a poster stating, "Paranormal investigator: the only job where asking, 'Is anybody here?' is considered professional communication." Norman's faint, pencil-thin mustache was his latest attempt to make his boyish face look older, but it only served as another source of amusement for Kat, who taunted him relentlessly about it.

"Aw, come on, Normie," Kat teased, her voice dripping with sarcasm as she eyed his mustache. "I thought you were growing out your facial hair to impress the spirits, not scare them away."

"Very funny, Skittles," Norman replied without looking up from his book, using the nickname he'd given Kat because of her colorful makeup. "Some of us are actually trying to improve our understanding of the paranormal."

Perched on the corner of Normie's desk, Kat's striking appearance contrasted sharply with the mismatched decor of the room. Her petite frame barely reached over five feet tall, but her boisterous, unfiltered personality more than compensated for her size. A halo of dim light seemed to illuminate her pale skin, and her heavy makeup accentuated her dark, mischievous eyes. Shoulder-length black hair, reminiscent of pin-up girls from a bygone era, framed her face, and long straight-cut bangs covered her forehead. She wore a t-shirt that boldly declared: "PARANORMAL INVESTIGATOR BECAUSE FREAKIN' AWESOME IS NOT AN OFFICIAL JOB TITLE."

Leaning forward, she inspected the thick book in Norman's hands, eager to give him a hard time. "Normie, are you sure you're not just summoning the ghosts of boredom past with that book?" she quipped, her dark eyes dancing mischievously.

Norman's head snapped up, his glasses slipping precariously down his nose. "Kat, this is serious research. I'm looking for rational explanations for our findings. You know, scientific rigor."

Kat snorted, her brightly painted red lips curling into a smirk. "Scientific rigor? How do you scientifically explain that pathetic thing you call a mustache?"

Huffing, Normie pushed his glasses back up his nose and glanced towards Chris. "Chris, I know *you* appreciate the true essence of spectral phenomena. Maybe we should do more investigating, so we aren't just left with these ghost walks, and tourists seeking cheap thrills."

"Normies right, Chris," Kat rolled her eyes dramatically. "Maybe we should hand out Ouija boards and glow sticks tonight for extra ambiance, you know, get a little *real* spirit activity going."

"Let's not undermine the integrity of our tours, guys," Chris raised an eyebrow, torn between amusement and concern.

"Fine, I'll leave the Ouija boards for another night." Kat let out an exaggerated sigh, her brashness softened by a playful smile.

"Alright, you two, which way do we want to head on the tour tonight - east or west. Any feeling where there might be some activity?" Chris interjected, hoping the change of subject would quiet the bickering.

Kat leaned back, crossing her arms. "Yeah, yeah, the monthly parade of skeptics hoping to catch a glimpse of Casper. My Ouija board says we go west."

Norman adjusted his glasses. "If you want an opportunity to educate the public about the intricacies of paranormal research, I think east of the courthouse might make for some interesting conversations."

"Sure, Normie. You want to talk and i want to see some *real* ghosts," Kat waved a hand dismissively.

"Let's not forget, people are interested in what we do. We've got a reputation to uphold," Chris chuckled, attempting to maintain order.

"Hey, east or west, I'm just hoping to add a touch of spectral elegance to the mix," Kat winked at Chris, striking a playful pose that accentuated her beauty.

"Ghostly elegance? Is that a new chapter in your paranormal fashion guide?" Norman sighed, rolling his eyes.

"Normie, my man, you do know that reading ancient scrolls won't summon a ghost, right?" Kat's voice dripped with sarcasm.

"Unlike your 'summoning ghosts with lipstick' technique, I prefer to rely on knowledge and evidence," Norman shot her an irritated glance, his dry sense of humor evident even in his exasperation.

Chris intervened before things could escalate further. "Can we please just focus on the tour?" he asked in an exasperated tone.

"Fine," Kat relented, crossing her arms over her chest. "But I still think we should do something exciting during the tour, like a séance or something."

"Absolutely not," Chris said firmly, his gaze locked on Kat. "We've talked about this before. We're not going to use cheap gimmicks to entertain our guests."

"Alright, alright," she sighed, rolling her eyes once more. "But if we end up with another group of yawning tourists, don't say I didn't warn you."

"Trust me, Kat," Chris replied, a hint of amusement in his voice. "I think our work speaks for itself."

"Speaking of work, Chris," Kat quickly chimed in, "when are we going to do some *real* paranormal investigating? I can't remember the last time I got goose bumps from a spook hunt." Kat leaned forward, placing her hands squarely on Chris's desk hoping to force the issue.

"Well, Kat, we've actually got a couple of people coming in this afternoon that might have an interesting story or two to tell," Chris flashed a wry smile.

"Ooooo... details please," Kat's eyes grew big and she leaned in expectantly.

"I spoke with a woman this morning who said she's had a few paranormal encounters in the past few days... seems both she and her daughter have seen the spirit of a little girl in their house."

"*Seen it?!*" Kat screeched, before turning to Norman with another snide remark. "Maybe you can take notes, Professor Mustache."

"Okay, enough," Chris said, trying to redirect the conversation back to their upcoming tour. "Focus, people. We have work to do."

"Ugh, fine," Kat grumbled, tossing her hair with an exaggerated pout. "But I'm more excited to meet with the two freaked-out people who've seen a real ghost."

"Let's not get ahead of ourselves," Norman cautioned, his brow furrowing as he double-checked the batteries in his infrared camera. "First, we need to hear their story and assess whether a full-scale investigation is warranted."

"Always the skeptic, huh, Normie?" Kat teased, nudging him playfully.

"Someone has to keep you grounded, Skittles," he replied, a hint of a smile tugging at the corners of his mouth.

As they continued their good-natured ribbing, Chris couldn't help but feel a surge of affection for his team. They may have their differences, but ultimately, they were united in a quest for knowledge and understanding. Chris looked forward to meeting Samantha and Maddie, feeling a renewed sense of purpose.

"Alright, guys," he called out, catching Kat and Normie's attention as he stood up from his desk. "Let's get ready for our guests."

Chapter Four

Is This The Right Place?

Maddie and I stared at the Georgetown Café and Bakery Shop on King Street. The charming building's worn brick walls, adorned with vintage posters, seemed to whisper secrets of bygone days.

"Is this the right place?" Maddie asked, her voice quiet and questioning. Her hand, so fragile and delicate, tightened around mine as if grasping for reassurance.

"I think so." I glanced down at my phone, double-checking the address, and furrowed my brow. "This is the address Chris gave me," I murmured, more to myself than to Maddie. We were supposed to find the office of the Leesburg Ghost Tours, but instead, we were greeted by the sight of a small café, its entrance offering no indication of any connection.

"Maybe it's inside?" Maddie suggested.

I shrugged, unsure of what else to do.

My thumb hovered above the screen of my phone. Chris's number was visible and ready to dial, but doubts gnawed at me. What if they didn't believe us? Or worse, just blew us off because they thought we were crazy?

"I'll give him a call," I mumbled, tapping the phone screen, and holding it to my ear. The line clicked, and the same quirky recording I'd heard earlier began to play. I waited for the beep, then left a brief message explaining our predicament.

"Hi, this is Samantha. My daughter Maddie and I are outside the address you gave, but it seems to be a café. Could you call me back and let us know where to meet you?"

I lowered the phone and glanced around, scanning the street for any signs of our mysterious paranormal investigators. Within minutes, the door to the café swung open, revealing two figures who were clearly the ones we'd been looking for.

"Hi there!" a young woman chirped, "I'm Katrina, but you can call me Kat!" Her voice bubbled with enthusiasm as she walked towards us. A small petite girl, she was the epitome of a pinup bombshell, her dark hair styled in victory rolls and her crimson lipstick perfectly applied. Beside her, a tall lanky man about my age moved with a more reserved air, his focus on the unusual-looking camera he held in his hands. "That's Normie," Kat continued, "Ignore him, please." Norman nodded a quick greeting and began circling us, capturing the scene with his odd camera from all angles.

"You must be Sam and Maddie!" Kat exclaimed, her words tumbling out in a cascade of exuberance. "Sorry about the confusion. We don't exactly have a traditional office setup to conduct interviews. So, tell me about this ghostly little girl you've encountered."

Questions tumbled from Kat's lips like a flood, and I instinctively drew Maddie closer to me, my mind grappling with the surge of emotions brought on by the sudden inquisition.

"Mommy, what's happening?" Maddie whispered, her small hand gripping mine tightly as she looked up at me with wide, curious eyes.

"Shh, it's okay," I reassured her, trying to keep my own composure as the whirlwind of questions continued. Just when I thought I couldn't take any more, a deep voice sliced through the chatter, ending Kat and Norman's antics.

"Alright, team, let's give them some breathing room," the authoritative voice commanded, and all heads turned toward the source. There, standing in the doorway of the café, was Chris - the lead paranormal investigator.

His tall, well-built frame radiated confidence, and his piercing blue eyes held an air of intrigue that captivated me instantly. He offered me a reassuring smile as he approached, extending a hand for me to shake.

"Nice to meet you in person, Samantha," he said smoothly, his gaze never leaving mine. "I'm Chris Janney."

"I'm Sam... nice to meet you, Chris," I stammered, all eloquence abandoning me in the face of his charm.

Maddie peeked out from behind me and offered a shy wave. Chris bent down and warmly greeted her.

"Hey there, what's your name?" he asked, his tone gentle and inviting.

"Maddie," she replied, a hint of shyness evident in her voice.

"Well, Maddie, it's nice to meet you too." His voice resonated in the air, like a blanket of warmth surrounding us. He offered his hand to Maddie, and she hesitantly shook one finger. Chris straightened up and his eyes returned to mine.

"How 'bout we find a more comfortable place to chat? The benches by the courthouse should do the trick. It's much more comfortable than my office, I can assure you."

My gaze followed his gesture to the courthouse square just over a block away. Maddie tugged at my hand, urging me to follow as Chris turned to lead us down the street. I took a deep breath and followed, captivated by the presence of the strikingly handsome man who led the way. Kat and Norman followed a short distance behind, chattering away as they engaged in playful banter.

We found a secluded spot under a sprawling oak tree, its massive branches providing a comforting canopy above us. Maddie and I took a seat on a rugged, worn-out bench that was surrounded by a bed of dry leaves. Chris arranged himself beside us with practiced ease, his presence serving as a reassuring anchor. Kat, eagerly maneuvered to a conspicuous spot directly in front of us, plopping herself down cross-legged on the ground. Norman, seemingly unfazed by us settling on the benches, drifted in a slow, unhurried orbit around us.

"First and foremost, Samantha," Chris began, his voice soft yet commanding, "I want you to know that you can speak freely. We're here to listen, not to judge." His eyes locked onto mine, a genuine sincerity evident in their deep blue depths. A warmth spread through me as our gazes met, and I nodded, my apprehension beginning to fade under his calming demeanor.

"Alright," I began, my voice steadier than I expected it to be, "where should I start?"

"Anywhere you feel comfortable," Chris replied.

I hesitated for a moment, my fingers tightly gripping the edge of the bench as I collected my thoughts. Maddie leaned against me, the weight of her presence both comforting and reassuring.

"Alright," I began, my voice steady despite the nervousness I felt. "We've only been in the house for a few days, but things started happening right away. It seems like Maddie has been the most affected by it all." My gaze drifted to my daughter's face. "She told me about a new friend she's been playing with - a little girl named Amelia."

"The ghost girl!" Kat interjected, her enthusiasm spilling out in a vibrant burst. She quickly caught herself, pressing her fingertips to her lips in an apologetic gesture. "Sorry... please continue" she whispered, her eyes still dancing with excitement. Maddie giggled at Kat's antics, her laughter a welcome contrast to the tension I felt.

Chris gave Kat a stern look before turning his attention to Maddie. "Can you tell me about Amelia, Maddie? How did you meet her?"

Maddie's eyes sparkled as she recounted her dreams of Amelia, her voice soft and wistful.

"In my dreams, we play together. Amelia tells me that she's lonely and sad. She says she needs help."

"You've only seen her in dreams?" Chris asked.

"No... she gets in bed with me sometimes, and she took

me to play in the yard." Chris nodded, then turned his attention to me.

"Have you experienced anything yourself, Samantha?"

I nodded, swallowing the lump that had formed in my throat. "Yes, I have. I saw the figure of a little girl in the bathroom mirror, and when I entered the room, there was this bitter cold."

"Funnel Apparition," Norman blurted out as he continued to film us and our surroundings. He looked up abruptly, realizing he had inadvertently broken the silence. Clearing his throat, he continued, "A Funnel Ghost is typically associated with older homes or historic buildings. They often appear with a cold spot nearby. Most paranormal research suggests they might be a returning loved one or a former resident."

Kat couldn't contain herself, her arms shooting up in excitement as she cheered, "Spook!" before quickly correcting herself with a playful gesture of locking her lips. The infectious sound of Maddie's laughter filled the air once more, inviting a smile to form on my lips. "Please, continue, Sam," Chris urged, nudging me gently with his words. His voice was a soothing balm against the turmoil of emotions that simmered inside me, and I took a deep breath before answering.

"There were other occurrences too," I began, my words unfolding like a map into the mysteries that had haunted our new home. "Cupboard doors in the kitchen opening and closing by themselves, shadows dancing on the walls at night without a light source to make them... and the TV turning on by itself."

Norman's lips move silently, mouthing the word "Poltergeist" before Chris shot him an icy glare, stopping him instantly.

"Go on," Chris encouraged.

I continued, my voice unwavering despite the interruption, describing how the TV would mysteriously turn on by itself and display an old black-and-white TV show.

Maddie piped up, her voice filled with youthful enthusiasm, "Ladies and gentlemen, welcome to the Lawrence Laine Starlight Revue!" Maddie mimicked the style of the show's introduction, her voice fluctuating with the same cadence as the announcer she had heard.

A warm smile spread across my face as. "Yes, that's right, Maddie. Whenever the TV comes on by itself, it's always playing that show."

"Interesting," Chris mused, his curiosity roused. "And where exactly is the old farmhouse located?"

"Old Waterford Road," I replied, giving him the details, and watching as Chris pulled out his phone to look up the address. He suddenly let out a low whistle, clearly taken back by the information on his screen.

"Would you look at that?" Chris murmured, almost to himself. "Your farmhouse sits adjacent to the old Lawrence Laine estate."

"Really?" Norman asked, surprise cutting through his usual dry demeanor. He opened his phone to confirm Chris's revelation. Kat sat quietly, her eyes wide and jaw dropped, visibly shocked by the news.

"Could that be why we're experiencing these...

hauntings?" I asked, searching Chris's eyes for an answer.

"Perhaps," he replied thoughtfully. "It could certainly explain the connection to the TV show." The strange occurrences in our home suddenly seemed to have a tangible link to the past.

"Poltergeist," Norman muttered again, unable to contain himself any longer. Chris shot him another disapproving glance, but it was clear that Norman's enthusiasm had gotten the best of him.

"Have there been any other experiences since you moved into the farmhouse?" Chris asked, his voice gentle yet insistent, a subtle challenge for me to dig deeper.

I hesitated for a moment, my mind replaying the eerie occurrences that had haunted our days and nights. "Well, there's the crying," I murmured, my gaze drifting to the ground as I recalled the plaintive wails that seemed to echo through the night air. "We hear it outside the house, and one night, I found Maddie standing in the front yard with the girl... they're about the same age."

"Really?" Chris's eyes widened, a flicker of concern passing across his face.

"Fireflies," Maddie interjected, her voice a bright contrast to the somber conversation. "they're always around Amelia and me when we're together."

I nodded, remembering the ethereal dance of the fireflies as they flitted through the darkness. "It concerns me that the spirit led Maddie outside at night," I confessed, feeling a shiver run down my spine.

"Interactive Personality apparitions!" Norman blurted out, momentarily setting aside his camera. He leaned in, eager to share his knowledge. "This form of spirit is common, usually a deceased historical figure. Sometimes friendly, sometimes not. They can become visible, speak, make noises, and even touch you. Experts believe this type of spirit can display a personality and even have emotions, often appearing to comfort or convey important information."

"Holy crap," Kat whispered, her eyes wide with shock. Chris merely nodded, acknowledging the unusual nature of our experiences.

"Mama, tell Chris about the toys," Maddie urged, her eyes shining with excitement.

"Right." I took a deep breath, steeling myself as I recalled the events that transpired earlier that day. "Maddie had a dream last night where Amelia took her to see her toys in the barn. This morning, we went into the barn and found the toys and a book, just as Maddie had described in her dream. Maddie even knew what the book was about before we found it."

"Whoa!" Kat exclaimed, falling over backward in disbelief.

Norman sputtered, his composure slipping away. "We have to conduct a proper investigation!"

"Alright, everyone, let's calm down," Chris said, his voice steady and reassuring. "I think it's best if my team heads back to the office to prepare for tonight's tour while I finish up our conversation here."

Chris gave Norman and Kat a gesture to indicate that it was time for them to go, and they slowly began to walk back down the street towards the cafe.

"Um, Chris," I began hesitantly, feeling a flush creeping across my face. "I'm not sure if you believe any of this or...or if you're just humoring us." I suddenly felt embarrassed for sharing our experiences, fearing that maybe he thought they were trivial."

"Please don't think that way," Chris said gently, his deep blue eyes locking onto mine. "I appreciate you sharing with us. You're right to be worried about the spirit leading Maddie outside at night. That's very unusual." Chris's brow furrowed with concern. "I agree with Norman... there's something unusual going on, and I think a proper investigation is warranted." He paused, allowing his words to sink in. "Would that be okay with you?"

"Y-yes," I stammered, relief washing over me.

"Great," Chris replied, his smile warm and reassuring. "We'll arrange a time when we can stay overnight at the farmhouse and conduct a thorough investigation, the sooner the better."

"Can you help Amelia?" Maddie asked, her small voice filled with concern. "I don't want her to be sad anymore."

"Maybe," Chris said gently, his gaze softening as he looked at my daughter. "We'll see if she'll talk to us, and then figure out if there's a way we can help."

"We'd appreciate that," I responded, squeezing Maddie's hand gently.

"Of course... and speaking of tonight," he continued, a hint of shyness creeping into his voice. "I was wondering if you'd like to join me on the tour. It would give us a chance to get to know each other better, and you might find it interesting."

"Um, well," I hesitated, glancing at Maddie. "I'm not sure about leaving her alone, and she needs her rest."

"She can stay with Kat back at the office while we're out. She'll be safe and well entertained there, I'm sure. Would you like that, Maddie?"

"Can I, Mama?" Maddie pleaded, "Kat's really funny!"

"Alright," I agreed, unable to resist the twinkle in her eyes. "As long as it's okay with Kat."

"Fantastic," Chris replied, his smile broadening as he stood up and extended a hand. A jolt of adrenaline surged through me s our fingers touched, leaving me a bit breathless and dizzy.

We started walking in the direction of the office with Chris once again leading the way. He talked about what I should expect on the tour, and explained the different types of hauntings he would be discussing. There was still so much I didn't understand, but I found myself drawn to Chris for who he was, not what he knew. I could figure all of that out later.

I couldn't help but notice a crowd had already gathered outside the Georgetown café.

"They're here early tonight," Chris remarked, "The tour doesn't start until eight."

I studied the people waiting and realized that most, if not all, were women. With a clipboard in hand, Kat moved gracefully among them, conversing with each and ticking off names. Around her neck, a loose arrangement of glow sticks emitted an enigmatic green glow.

"Hey, everyone," Chris called out as we approached the crowd. The women flocked around him instantly, giggling and blushing like teenagers. It was obvious they were more interested him than they were about seeing ghosts. A twinge of jealousy tugged at my heart, but I quickly pushed it aside.

"Chris," Kat said, turning towards him, "everyone who reserved a spot on the tour is here."

He checked his watch and addressed the group. "Well, since we're all here early, would you guys be okay with starting the tour now? We could extend it a bit, cover both the east and west routes since we have the extra time."

The group excitedly agreed. I noticed, however, that the one or two men present seemed skeptical. They exchanged amused glances, as if they were just along for the ride, not expecting anything extraordinary.

"Alright then, let's get started," Chris announced, his voice confident and commanding. The women in the crowd hung on his every word, their gazes fixated on him as though he held the key to unlocking the mysteries of the universe. I shook my head, amused by their fascination, and yet, I couldn't deny the magnetic pull he had on me as well.

Norman stepped forward, holding a strange assortment of equipment in his hands. He launched into a detailed explanation of each, his voice enthusiastic and filled with passion for the subject.

"Now, this here is an EMF detector," he said, brandishing a small device that looked like a cross between a walkie-talkie and a Star Trek prop. "It measures electromagnetic fields, which can sometimes indicate paranormal activity. You'll see – "

"Not every spike in EMF means we're dealing with a ghost," Chris interrupted. "Old wiring, electronics, even cell phones can cause false readings. But if something seems unusual, we'll have Norman check it out. "

"Right," Norman agreed before moving on to explain the other gadgets he had brought along.

Chris turned to Kat, who was standing nearby. "Hey, Kat, would you mind keeping an eye on Maddie while Sam and I go on the tour? She can hang out with you in the office."

Kat rolled her eyes dramatically, feigning disappointment. "Oh, darn. And I was just *so* looking forward to going on another ghost tour," she said sarcastically, but her tone quickly shifted to one of warmth as she walked over and took Maddie's hand. "Come on, kiddo, let's go have some fun." Maddie's eyes sparkled with excitement, and they vanished into the bustling café.

"Stay close by me, Sam," Chris said softly.

Other women were jockeying for a closer position, and I pushed past them. I wasn't about to let them crowd me out.

"Alright everyone, gather 'round," Chris announced, a wicked grin on his face as he looked at the eager crowd. I couldn't help but be drawn in by the intoxicating energy. "Tonight, we'll delve into the mysteries of Leesburg's haunted past, exploring stories that have been whispered through generations."

"Ooh, maybe we'll see a ghost!" one woman yelled, her friends giggling nervously.

"Who knows, it's happened before," Chris replied with a playful wink, causing a flutter of whispers among the women. Even the skeptical men seemed to be more engaged by Chris's confident charisma.

"Our first stop will be just down the street, where an old Victorian mansion is said to harbor several restless spirits. Follow me closely and don't hesitate to ask questions or share your own experiences."

As we began our walk, Chris moved closer to me so we could talk.

"Leesburg has a rich history of paranormal activity," Chris explained, his voice filled with passion. "Many of these stories can be traced back to the Civil War, when this area was right in the thick of it."

"Really?" I asked, genuinely intrigued. "I had no idea."

"Growing up here, you hear all sorts of tales," he said, giving me a warm smile. "The Battle of Ball's Bluff, for example, was a brutal fight that left countless soldiers dead... and ghosts haunting the battlefield. Then there's the Tally Ho Theater here in town, where the spirit of an old groundskeeper is said to still be watching over the place."

The way Chris spoke made it clear that he was deeply connected to the town, and I found myself wanting to learn more.

"How did you get into this line of work?" I asked, genuinely curious.

"It's hard not to be fascinated by the paranormal," he replied. "I've always been drawn to the unknown... the idea that there's more to this world than meets the eye. When I started investigating, I found that some stories were nothing more than old wives' tales. But others..."

He trailed off, looking at his surroundings thoughtfully. "Others turned out to be very real. Be right back." Chris nodded and made his way to the front of the crowd.

"Just a little further up here, that big house up ahead. Hang close, everyone."

I realized I was growing more interested in Chris, he *was* very attractive. I watched as the muscles shifted beneath his shirt. I noticed the determined set of his jaw, and the intensity in his eyes when he spoke to the crowd. It all served to draw me closer, both physically and emotionally.

"Here we are," Chris said, stopping in front of a beautiful but slightly dilapidated house, its peeling paint and overgrown garden adding an air of mystery. He began recounting a story of lost love, betrayal, and murder. The emotion in his voice made the story seem very real.

We bounced from location to location, exploring the dark corners and hidden secrets of Leesburg. Chris made sure to stay close, chatting away as we moved from one haunted place to the next.

"Promise me something," I asked as we walked past an old cemetery, the sound of laughter echoing around us. "When this is all over... the tour and all... promise you'll sit down and talk with me... you know... *really* talk."

Chris looked at me and nodded, his eyes filled with a mixture of surprise and warmth. "I'd like that very much," he said softly, reaching out to squeeze my hand.

The moon was shining brightly as we arrived at the Glenfiddich House. Chris paused at the wrought-iron gate, and turned to address the group.

"Welcome to Harrison Hall, better known as the

Glenfiddich House," he announced, his voice hushed and reverential. "This beautiful building has a dark past, haunted by the restless spirit of Col. Erasmus Burt."

Chris went on to describe the tragic tale of the injured Confederate soldier who had been brought to this house after the Battle of Ball's Bluff. He later succumbed to his wounds and died in the mansion.

"Those who've stayed here or worked within these walls have encountered many strange things," Chris stated, his voice barely above a whisper. "Unknown voices in hallways when no one was around, the sounds of shuffling footsteps from empty rooms... they've all been heard in this house. Some even claim to have seen the ghost of Col. Burt himself, forever lingering in the place where he drew his last breath."

A collective shudder ran through the group, and I smiled.

"Hey, Samantha!" a voice called out from behind me, pulling me abruptly from my thoughts. I turned to see the store attendant I had interviewed just the day before. "How's your magazine article coming along?"

"Um, it's... started," I admitted, feeling a little disoriented by her sudden appearance. "I've had a lot on my plate the past couple of days, so I haven't gotten much done."

"Ah, well, I'm sure you'll get around to it. What brings you to the ghost tour?"

"Actually, I was just wondering the same about you," I replied, genuinely curious.

She laughed, a musical sound that seemed strangely out of place. "Oh, I haven't missed one of these tours in months! Chris is quite the storyteller – and easy on the eyes, too, don't you think?" She nudged me playfully, and I couldn't help but smile.

"Can't argue with that," I agreed, casting a sideways glance at our enigmatic tour guide.

As the tour continued, Chris and I spoke briefly between stops. "I was wondering if you noticed," he said, his voice gentle, "Some of the things I've pointed out are similar to what you've experienced at the farmhouse."

"Yeah, I'm starting to see the similarities," I admitted. "I kinda new they were paranormal in nature, but it's interesting to hear that others have seen the same."

"We'll know more after the investigation." Chris concluded.

We ended the tour at the Leesburg courthouse, near the benches where Maddie and I had spoken with Chris and his team.

" This tour has been... enlightening, to say the least," I said as we stood beneath the courthouse's towering façade.

Chris smiled, his eyes crinkling at the corners. "I'll trust that's a good thing. I'm glad you enjoyed it.

The night air was cool as we made our way back to the Georgetown café. We entered and climbed the stairs to the team's one-room office, quickly opening the door. Maddie and Kat sat cross-legged on the floor, playing with a Ouija board. The flickering candlelight cast eerie shadows across their faces, making the scene look like something out of a horror movie.

"Think that's a good idea, Kat?" Chris asked, a note of concern in his voice.

Kat looked up, her dark eyes gleaming. "Oh, come on,"

she scoffed. "We kept it light, didn't we kiddo?"

Maddie nodded, her eyes wide with excitement. "It was fun! Kat asked the game lots of questions about me and Amelia, huh, Kat?"

"Research." Kat replied, a mischievous grin spreading across her face.

The door to the office opened behind us and Norman entered the room, looking utterly exhausted. He practically collapsed into a chair, running a hand through his disheveled hair. Maddie stared at him for a moment before Kat gave her a nudge and silently mouthed the words, "Ask him."

"Normie, what's that on your lip?" she asked. "It looks like you've been drinking chocolate milk!"

I stifled a laugh, covering my mouth with my hand. Kat, however, completely lost it. She doubled over with laughter, tears streaming down her cheeks.

"God, I love this girl!" she yelled between gasps for air, referring to Maddie. "You're absolutely right, kid, that pathetic excuse for a moustache looks *exactly* like chocolate milk!"

Norman frowned and protested weakly, trying to sound indignant but failing to hide the embarrassment in his voice. "Hey, it's a work in progress!"

With a final round of laughter echoing behind us, Maddie, Chris, and I made our way down the stairs and to the street outside the café. The night sky was a deep shade of indigo, the air crisp and cool.

"Did you have fun with Kat?" I asked Maddie, watching her eyes sparkle as she nodded enthusiastically.

"Yeah, she's funny! And the Ouija board was interesting."

"Interesting, huh? We'll have to talk more about that later." I ruffled her hair affectionately, then turned to Chris.

"Thanks again for taking me on the tour, Chris," I said, my voice unexpectedly soft. "Your knowledge about the history and hauntings is really impressive."

"Hey, it was my pleasure," he replied, flashing a smile that gave me butterflies. "Any excuse to spend time with you guys is a good one." His words hung in the air between us, charged with unspoken meaning. "Anyway," Chris cleared his throat, breaking the spell. "I'll give you a call tomorrow to schedule the investigation."

"Sounds good," I replied, my heart racing from our momentary connection.

"Take care, you two," Chris said warmly as he turned to leave.

"Night, Chris," Maddie chimed in, waving as he walked away.

"Goodnight," I echoed, struggling to keep the emotion from my voice.

I took Maddie's hand and led her away from the café, silently allowing myself to entertain a single, fragile hope: that maybe, just maybe, love could be the light that guided us to better things.

Chapter Five
Spiders and Pizza

Maddie sat at the kitchen table, her tiny hands resting in her lap as she patiently waited for me to bring her breakfast.

"Are you sure this is all you want?" I asked as I grabbed a bowl from the cupboard and opened the box of Maddie's favorite cereal. "I can slice up a banana to put on it if you want."

"Just cereal." Maddie replied.

The sound of the cereal pouring into the bowl was drowned out by a sharp screech; the sound a chair would make if pushed on a hard surface.

"Are you going somewhere?" I asked before glancing back at Maddie, expecting to see her standing. Maddie hadn't moved. She remained in her seat, her eyes fixed on the empty chair that had moved away from the table across from her.

"Did you push that chair out with your feet?" I asked, hoping for a logical explanation.

Maddie shook her head, her curls bouncing with the motion. "It just moved on its own," she said softly, her voice filled with wonder.

Taking a deep breath, I crossed the room with Maddie's cereal and placed it in front of her. I cautiously pushed the empty chair back under the table and returned to the kitchen to pour myself a cup of coffee. The hairs on the back of my neck stood on end as I heard the screeching noise again. I turned to see the chair pulled back once more, as though someone or something, had taken a seat. Maddie was grinning, clearly amused by the situation.

"Looks like we have a guest," I said, walking back to the table. Sitting down beside Maddie, I tried to make light of the situation. "I guess Amelia will be joining us for breakfast."

"Yep, guess so," Maddie giggled, her eyes sparkling with amusement as she ate a spoonful of cereal. I couldn't help but marvel at her ability to find joy in even the strangest circumstances. I took a sip of my coffee, feeling its warmth spread through my body. My cell phone vibrated, the number for the Ghost Tour flashing on the screen. Wiping my mouth with a napkin, I answered, "Hello?"

"Hey Sam, it's Chris." I thought his voice sounded warm and inviting. "I was calling to schedule our investigation at the farmhouse. Have you experienced any more activity since we last spoke?"

"Actually, we're having an event right now," I replied, glancing over at the mysteriously pulled-out chair. "Amelia seems to have joined Maddie and me for breakfast this morning."

"Really?" Chris chuckled. "That's amusing. I think it's important that we do the investigation tonight while the activity is strong, that is... if you're ok with it."

"Sounds good to me," I agreed, feeling a mixture of excitement and apprehension. "What time should we expect you?"

"Would 5 o'clock work? We'll need some time to set up our equipment and get familiar with the surroundings."

"That works," I responded, quickly checking my phone to figure out how much time I had before we needed to be ready.

"Great! Oh, and I thought I'd bring some pizzas for dinner, if that sounds ok." His offer brought a smile to my face, grateful for the kindness he showed us.

"Absolutely. Maddie loves pizza."

"Perfect. We'll see you later." With that, we ended the call.

"Guess what?" I asked, turning to Maddie who was still giggling at Amelia's antics. "Chris, Norman, and Kat are coming over tonight to spend the night with us. They're going to help us learn more about Amelia."

"Really?!" Maddie's face lit up with a smile that quickly morphed into a frown. "Amelia doesn't want anyone else here."

I raised my eyebrows, taken aback by her sudden change in mood. "Well, Amelia needs to know that it's just for one night." Maddie hesitated for a moment, then nodded. Realizing that Amelia might be in the room, I turned to the empty chair. "Amelia," I said softly, "the people coming tonight will be here to help you. You don't need to be afraid of them."

Maddie's face twisted in a scowl; her small fists clenched

on the table. "Amelia doesn't want anyone else's help. She wants *me* to help her. She doesn't trust anyone else."

"Sweetheart," I sighed, stroking her hair gently, "I understand that Amelia is scared, but we can't do this alone. Chris and his team know what they're doing. They'll be careful and respectful, I promise. It's just for one night."

The words had barely left my lips when a glass flew across the kitchen, hurtling from the counter to smash against the wall. Gasping, I stared at the shattered remains before turning to look at Maddie and the empty chair. Maddie's eyes were wide, but she didn't seem frightened. If anything, she was amused.

"Alright, Amelia," I said as I moved to clean up the mess, "That's not very nice. We're trying to help you, so please, no more tantrums, okay?" The sternness in my voice was tempered with an undercurrent of compassion. I couldn't bring myself to be truly angry with this lost soul.

A giggle bubbled up from Maddie and she nodded at me. "Okay, Samantha," Maddie said grinning, her voice noticeably deeper. "I just wanted to make sure you knew how I felt."

"Maddie?" I gasped in disbelief, visibly shaken. Was it possible that the voice I'd heard was Amelia's, coming from Maddie?

"She's sorry, Mommy, Maddie answered, her voice now in her familiar tone. "She'll try to behave."

"Thank you," I replied, feeling uneasy yet glad that the atmosphere seemed calmer. The sound of breaking glass still echoed in my ears, a sharp reminder of how fragile our circumstances had become. As I swept up the shards of broken glass, I couldn't help but wonder what the night would bring. Would Amelia cooperate, or would her fear drive her to act out even more?

The sun was beginning its descent when Chris, Norman, and Kat arrived at the farmhouse. The evening light painted the sky in warm hues, casting a soft glow on their faces as they climbed out of the van. Maddie waved excitedly as we greeted them.

"Welcome," I said, smiling warmly. "Maddie and I have been looking forward to you coming."

"Thanks, Samantha," Chris replied, his eyes meeting mine. "We're eager to see what this place has to offer. Ready to show us around?"

"Of course," I nodded, and motioned for them to follow me. Maddie eagerly took the lead, apparently forgetting Amelia's anxiety at having guests in the house.

I led them through each room, recounting the various events that had taken place. In Maddie's bedroom, I showed them the bathroom mirror where I had seen the little girl. They seemed to curiously take in every little detail, and frequently asked questions.

In the family room, I pointed out the television that had a mind of its own. Maddie chimed in with tales of her own encounters, dramatically explaining what had happened.

"Amelia and I watch TV together," she told them. "She thinks it's funny when I laugh at the old shows."

"Interesting," said Norman, clearly eager to investigate further.

"Let's head outside to the barn," I suggested, guiding the group through the kitchen and out the back door. We entered the barn with our guests, showing them where Maddie and I had discovered the hidden cache of toys. I watched as Chris, Norman, and Kat inspected the items, fascinated by their antiquity.

Leaving the barn, Chris noticed the entrance to the cellar by the back porch.

"Have either of you been down there?" he asked, curiously.

"Um, not yet. But I've been planning to explore it at some point. We just haven't really taken the time."

"Would you mind if we took a look now?" Chris asked. "It might help us get a better understanding of the house's layout."

"Sure," I agreed, watching as Norman pulled at the cellar doors. They creaked open to reveal a wooden stairway leading below. Kat, however, seemed less enthusiastic. Her eyes flickered with unease as she took in the dimly lit stairs.

"I'll stay up here with Maddie," she volunteered, her voice wavering slightly. Maddie nodded, happy to remain with Kat.

The air in the cellar was musty and damp, making me shiver as we descended the wooden stairs. As my eyes adjusted to the dim light, I took in the cluttered space around us. Old boxes, their contents spilling out, were strewn about haphazardly.

"Wow, look at all these," I murmured, tracing my fingers along the dusty ribbons that hung from the beams above us. They were awards for equestrian events - blue for first place finishes, red for second, and various other colors for the remaining places. "Someone must have been quite the rider."

Chris nodded, then turned to scan the stone walls of the cellar. "You know, this foundation is obviously older than the house itself. I think the farmhouse might have been built on top of an older home, maybe a log cabin from the late 1700s or early 1800s."

"Wow," I whispered, suddenly feeling the weight of history surrounding us.

I noticed an old washing machine tucked away in a corner. "Looks like they did laundry down here," I commented, running my hand along the pink-and-white rounded barrel of the antique device. The Kenmore washer boasted a wringer on top and various handles protruding from its sides. It was clearly a relic of the 1950s, and I couldn't help but smile at the thought of using it. "I doubt I'll be doing any laundry down here anytime soon, not with this anyway." We shared a laugh, the eerie atmosphere momentarily forgotten.

"Wait, did you hear that?" Chris admonished us asking for quiet. "Do you hear footsteps?" We froze in our tracks, listening intently as the faint padding of footsteps moved from one end of the beams above us to the other.

"I hear it, Norman whispered, and I nodded my confirmation as well.

"Kat," Chris called out, "is Maddie inside the house?"

"Nope," Kat responded nonchalantly, "she's right here next to me."

"I gotta check this out." Norman muttered before bounding towards the basement stairs.

"Watch out!" I cried, a little too late. Norman ran straight into a spider's web that stretched down from the beams above, and frantically began swiping at his face and hair.

"Aaaaaa!" Norman cried out, flailing as he spun around trying to rid himself of the sticky strands. His scream was high-pitched, almost comical, and he shuddered violently as he tried to disentangle himself.

"I hate spiders!" he gasped, his face a mix of disgust and annoyance.

Laughter echoed down from the top of the stairs where Kat stood. "Need some help there, Normie?" she called, an amused glint in her dark eyes.

"Are you going to come down here to help me?" Norman challenged her, trying to regain his dignity.

"Nope," she replied, giggling at his obvious discomfort. "You seem to have everything under control."

We made our way back upstairs, leaving the dusty basement and its eight-legged inhabitants behind. Norman ran up the porch steps and quickly entered the house, hoping to find the source for the footsteps we had just heard.

"We should get our equipment set up." Chris instructed Kat in a business like tone as he began walking towards the van.

"Let's eat the pizzas before they get cold, and then we can set everything up," suggested Kat, always eager for an opportunity to indulge in her favorite food.

"Right," said Chris, having forgotten about the dinner he'd brought. He slowed his walk, then stopped. "Let's eat first, then we'll work."

Kat smiled and feigned a knowing expression at Chris as she walked towards the van to retrieve the pizzas. Chris joined me, shrugging in compliance as we headed to the front porch, eager to relax and enjoy our dinner.

―――

Maddie snuggled close to my side, her eyes wide with delight as she enjoyed the delicious melted cheese on her slice of pizza. The sun had just set, casting a silvery glow across the surrounding fields. It seemed impossible to believe that this idyllic scene could be home to such mysterious events.

"Mama, can I go watch them set up the equipment?" Maddie asked, her gaze following Norman and Kat as they began to move around inside the house.

"I guess so, but stay out of the way, okay?" I replied, giving her a gentle squeeze.

"Promise!" she grinned and hurried off to join the investigators. Maddie eagerly followed Kat and Norman from room to room, peppering them with questions while they worked.

"Maddie seems really taken with all of this," I commented to Chris, noting the spark in her eyes that I hadn't seen in some time.

"Sometimes, the unknown can be a welcome distraction," he said, his voice soft and understanding.

The air was thick with the scent of blooming flowers, accompanied by a distant chirping of crickets. Chris and I sat side-by-side in the rockers, our hands unconsciously inching closer together as we spoke.

"Chris," I began, my voice soft, "tell me more about yourself. You promised on the tour, remember?"

"Ah, yes. I did, didn't I?" He gave me a small smile, his gaze shifting to the horizon as he gathered his thoughts.

"There isn't much to tell, really," he replied, rubbing the back of his neck as if slightly embarrassed. "I was born in Paeonian Springs, a small town just a few miles from here. My family has lived in Waterford and Leesburg for generations. We were some of the original settlers in the area."

"Wow," I said, genuinely intrigued. "So, you have deep roots here."

"Yeah, you could say that," he chuckled. "My great-great-grandfather, Amos Janney, built a mill on the south fork of Catoctin Creek in the mid 1700s. A small settlement grew around it, which eventually became the town of Waterford."

"Interesting," I commented, noticing the pride in his voice.

"Most of my family were big Quakers, very active in the religion. But I'm not really a religious person myself, and I don't keep up with distant relatives who are still involved."

"Fair enough," I nodded, understanding that everyone's spiritual journey is different.

Chris leaned forward, resting his elbows on his knees. "As for my love of the paranormal, it grew from stories my grandfather used to tell me." His voice took on a nostalgic tone as he continued. "He was fascinated by Civil War history and would tell me tales of ghostly encounters and haunted battlefields. I guess you could say it was his passion that sparked mine."

"Your grandfather sounds like he was an amazing man. He opened up a whole new world for you."

He was," Chris agreed, his eyes shining as he recalled distant memories.

"What kind of training do you have?" I asked, curious about how one becomes a paranormal investigator.

"Ah, well," he shifted in his seat, running a hand through his hair. "I've had some training and received credentials from various institutions, but no formal degrees. Paranormal studies are considered pseudoscience, not real scientific work. Still, I've learned a lot over the years, and I'm always eager to learn more."

"Your passion definitely shows," I said, admiring his dedication. "It's clear that you love what you do."

"Thanks, Sam," he replied, his eyes meeting mine with a smile. "I truly believe there's a lot we *don't* know about the universe around us. I just want to know more about some of those mysteries."

Feeling a sudden surge of vulnerability, I hesitated before asking my next question. "So, um, do you have someone special in your life... a love interest?" I blushed, embarrassed by my forwardness.

Chris looked surprised but smiled reassuringly. "I was

married once, actually. But it only lasted six years." His expression turned somber. "My work made paying the bills difficult, and it put a lot of pressure on our marriage. We eventually just drifted apart, with less and less in common." He sighed. "I haven't seen her or heard from her in years, not since she moved away."

Sam noticed Chris shift uncomfortably in his rocker, hesitating before he continued to speak.

"It's still difficult at times, financially. I mainly rely on the ghost tours and an occasional lecture or published article to make ends meet."

"Wait," I interjected, puzzled. "You said that your family was prominent. I assumed you inherited a portion the family's wealth."

Chris shook his head. "There is family money, but it's held in a trust and has stipulations about receiving payments. My family wanted descendants to be active members in the Quaker faith, which I'm not." He shrugged, a hint of dejection in his voice.

"Ah, I see," I murmured, sympathizing with his situation.

"Enough about me," Chris declared, changing the topic. "What about you and Maddie? Tell me more about you guys."

I took a deep breath and began, "Well, I was born in Florida, actually. My father was in the military, so we bounced around the country and lived all over the place because of him. I became pretty self-reliant because of it, I guess. I went to college, got my degree in journalism and ended up in New York, writing for magazine."

"That's awesome. Have I ever read any of your articles?"

"I doubt it," I replied with a small smile. "Most of my work has been regional pieces and exposés. My career is on hold now because of Maddie's illness." My heart grew heavy as I continued, "The publication I work for paid for the rental of this farmhouse so that Maddie and I could spend some time together."

Chris looked surprised when I mentioned Maddie was sick and his expression changed to one of genuine concern.

"There's something you should know about Maddie," I hesitated, my voice trembling slightly. "She's... she's terminally ill."

"Terminally?" His eyes widened in shock. "I noticed she was small for her age, but I never imagined - "

"Classic symptoms of her blood disease," I interrupted. "Small in stature with an overly large head for her body." The words were difficult to say, like dragging something through molasses. "Maddie bruises easily, sometimes even with the slightest touch. She's always tired and often has trouble breathing."

Chris' hand found mine, enveloping it in a warm, comforting embrace. "I can't imagine what you must be going through."

"Sometimes, the hardest battles are fought in silence," I whispered, my eyes glistening. I swallowed hard before continuing. "We tried a bone marrow transplant, but it didn't take. The doctors said... they said she only has a few months left." The tears finally broke free, streaming down my cheeks like hot rain.

Without hesitation, Chris pulled me into his arms,

enveloping me in a protective embrace. My heart raced, both from the distress of discussing Maddie's grim prognosis, and the undeniable attraction I felt. It was a strange and unexpected emotion, but one that I couldn't help but welcome. After a few moments, I composed myself and pulled back. "That's about all there is to tell about us," I said, attempting a weak smile.

"Sam, you're incredibly strong. You show such love and care for Maddie," Chris murmured, his admiration evident. "I just have one last question for you. It's only fair since you asked me the same thing earlier. Is there anyone special in your life besides Maddie? I mean, a love interest?"

A sad smile crossed my lips as I answered, "No, there's no one special in my life right now. Maddie's father... he died years ago. He was in the military, like my dad and we met in Iraq when I was there writing a story."

My thoughts drifted back to that whirlwind romance, so intense and passionate.

"He was our driver on the assignment, and we hit it off. We married a few months later, during a break from his deployment." Pausing for a moment, I took in a shaky breath before adding, "Maddie was born soon after, on the same day her dad... my husband, was killed."

The memory of that day was still raw, even after all these years.

"Sam, I'm so sorry," Chris whispered, his hand gently caressing mine. "Your husband... was he killed in combat?"

I shook my head. "No, oddly enough, it was a drunk driving accident."

I felt a familiar pang in my chest as I thought of the cruel twist of fate that had robbed Maddie of her father.

"Maddie never knew him, but she could always pick him out in photo albums when they were shown to her. She talked like she knew him – it was weird."

"Really?" Chris's eyebrows rose in surprise. "That's fascinating. Maybe she has some kind of spiritual gift, like a medium or something."

"Maybe," I mused, feeling a wistful longing stir within me. "I just wish she had the gift of healing, so she could make her illness go away."

"Sam, I'm not a religious person, but I believe that everyone has an inner light. It's an old Quaker belief, something they call the 'inward light.'" He paused, lost in thought for a moment before continuing. "Quakers believe that finding times of silence and stillness will enable us to feel the presence of God, which will, in turn, show us the reality about our lives, including what we need to be doing to fulfill God's will."

"Taking time to find silence and stillness... that sounds like a good thing to me, but I don't know about the rest. I can't imagine why it would be God's will that Maddie has to die... that just doesn't work for me."

"Maybe it doesn't have to work for you," Chris countered, "Maybe it's just the way things were meant to be. But if I were in your shoes, I'd definitely be listening to any voice that could bring me comfort... and purpose."

Without warning, the front door blasted open, and Norman and Kat stepped out onto the porch, their voices raised in a heated discussion. Norman clutched an EMF meter in one hand and a digital voice recorder in the other, his tall lanky frame tense with frustration. Kat's eyes flashed defiantly, her dark hair framing her pale face like a raven's wings.

"Chris, I swear, if you don't help me deal with Normie and his ridiculous theories about EMF detectors, I'm going to lose it," Kat's voice cut through the air like a knife, shattering my momentary serenity.

"Kat, I'm just saying that we need to be thorough and methodical in our approach," Norman stammered, adjusting his glasses nervously. "We can't just go around placing equipment haphazardly."

"Ok, guys, enough!" Chris interjected, rising from the rocking chair to stand between them. He gave me a quick, apologetic glance before turning to face his bickering teammates. "Let's all take a deep breath and discuss this calmly inside."

"Fine," Kat muttered, rolling her eyes as she followed Chris into the house. Norman trailed behind them, still stubbornly clinging to his equipment.

As the door closed behind them, I found myself alone on the porch once more. Their interruption had left me feeling a mixture of irritation and amusement, but as the silence settled around me again, I couldn't help but feel grateful for the brief distraction.

Tears prickled at the corners of my eyes, as I whispered a silent prayer into the night, willing the universe to give me a sign. Despite the fear and worry that still lingered in my heart, I couldn't help but feel a glimmer of hope... the faintest flicker of an inward light, waiting to be discovered.

Chapter Six

This Ain't Yo Mama's Ghost Tour

The air was thick with anticipation as I sat in the back of the beat-up van, huddled under a blanket. It was just past 3 a.m., and Maddie had been sleeping for hours. I made sure she was safely tucked-in and asleep before joining Chris, Norman, and Kat in the van. An uneasy quiet had settled over us as we sat watching monitors that displayed video streams from inside and around the farmhouse.

"These lightening-bugs are driving me crazy," Norman complained, adjusting his glasses. "It's hard to determine what's an insect and what's not."

"We'll have the recordings to go over tomorrow," Chris said trying to reassure Norman. "We won't miss anything."

The cameras were set up in the family room, the kitchen, Maddie's room, and both the exterior of the barn and the surrounding area, as well as the outside of the house looking up at Maddie's bedroom window. We had been watching for several hours, but there hadn't been any signs of activity. I was focused mostly on the feed from Maddie's room, where I could see her sleeping peacefully.

Kat began to snicker and covered her face with her hands.

"What's gotten into you, Kat?" Norman asked, raising an eyebrow.

"I think a spirit joined us." Kat responded, her hand covering her mouth as she attempted to contain the snickers that were building.

"Wait, what?" Norman grabbed his EMF meter and turned it on, hoping to find evidence of a spectral presence.

"I don't see any activ...," his voice ended abruptly as he wrinkled his nose. "What's that smell? Do you guys' smell that?"

"Maybe our spirit friend has a message for us," Kat responded, openly laughing now. "Who knows, ghosts have communicated in stranger ways, right?"

Chris rolled his eyes, glancing at me sheepishly before turning to exit out the back of the van. "I don't think that's a ghostly aroma, Kat." Within seconds we were standing in the darkness behind the van, Kat still chuckling and Norman pacing in obvious disgust.

"We needed that little break, I think." Chris's voice broke the amused silence between all of us. "I'd like to be a little more proactive anyway, I think."

Chris instructed Norman to grab a piece of equipment for him and remain in the van to record the session he'd just decided to conduct. After giving Kat a sideways glance, Norman reluctantly agreed and crawled back inside.

"See you in a few, Normie," Kat waved and pretended to pinch her nose as she followed us into the house.

As we made our way inside the dimly lit farmhouse, I couldn't help but shiver, feeling a bit of tension in the air. The family room seemed eerily still, as if waiting for something to happen. Chris made some adjustments to his device.

"What's that?" I asked, curious about the meter he was holding. Chris began explaining the equipment he was using, an Ovilus 5.

"This device scans environmental readings and correlates them with a list of words and phrases," he said, his voice low and serious. "It has precision sensors to detect changes in the environment, allowing ghosts to communicate more precisely. As a result, the Ovilus 5 can convert these readings into words, making it quick and easy for us to gather answers during investigations." He paused before adding, "It also has motion sensors to indicate the presence of a possible spirit."

Chris placed the device on the floor in the center of the room. It flashed, intermittently letting us know it was active. A voice crackled over our radio headsets as Norman's voice filled our ears. "Starting to record now."

"Alright, let's get started," Chris whispered in a quiet voice. "Amelia, if you're here with us, please make your presence known."

The air seemed to grow colder, more tense, but everything remained quiet.

"Is there anyone here who wishes to communicate with us?" Chris asked, his voice echoing through the empty room.

The motion sensors flickered lightly, suggesting some sort of presence in the room, but there was no clear message on the Ovilus screen.

"Maybe she's scared," Kat offered, her tone softening a little.

"Let's try again," I suggested, hoping we could find some answers for Amelia. "Amelia, we're here to help you. Please, talk to us."

The room remained quiet, and Chris sighed, running a hand through his hair as he picked up the device from the floor. "I'm going to let Norman take a look at this. Maybe I don't have it set up right."

The silence weighed heavily on us, and I couldn't help but feel a sense of despair settling in. What if Amelia had decided not to show herself tonight? I shook my head, refusing to let that thought take root. I knew Amelia was here. We just needed to wait for her.

"Let's head back to the van and regroup," Chris said quietly. "There's still more night ahead of us."

My eyelids felt heavier with each passing moment, my exhaustion finally catching up. I decided it was time to step away and try to get some rest.

"Chris, I'm going to call it a night and get some sleep. I need to be ready for Maddie when she wakes up."

Chris nodded in agreement and said good night. "I'll let you know if anything pops up."

Leaving Chris and Kat in the family room, I entered my bedroom and closed the door gently behind me, hoping for just a few hours of shut eye. As my head hit the pillow, scenes of Amelia and her tormented spirit filled my dreams, leaving me restless.

Chris and Kat continued their investigation after confirming with Norman that the device was working properly. They headed to the barn and made their way inside. They moved cautiously through the dimly lit structure, careful not to disturb any of the items scattered around the room. The air was still, with only the distant rustling of leaves and the gentle hum of insects breaking the silence.

"Amelia, are you here with us?" Chris asked, his voice reverberating slightly off the wooden walls. Everything was quiet, and the equipment screen remained blank. Chris repeated the question several more times, but every query brought the same results.

"Let's get back to the van," Chris suggested, disappointment evident in his voice. Within seconds of abandoning their session, Chris and Kat's radio headsets crackled to life.

"Chris, I'm picking ups some strange sounds. I think it might be activity," Norman reported, his excitement evident. The sensors were picking up something unusual... the sound of a little girl crying.

"We're on it," Chris responded, glancing at Kat as they exited the barn and walked to a nearby camera. They stood there quietly, listening for the sound Norman had picked up. A muffled scream was heard in the distance, followed by the sound of a little girl crying.

"That came from behind the barn... the pasture." Kat exclaimed, and Chris nodded in agreement. Together, they jogged in the direction of the sound.

Fireflies swirled above a small area of tall grass in the empty field. The glow of the insects cast eerie shadows as Chris and Kat cautiously approached. They could hear the crying intensify as they drew nearer the swarm.

"Look at this," Chris murmured, drawing Kat's attention to a crumbled stone structure beneath the throng of fireflies. It appeared to be the remains of a small building; its stones scattered on the ground like so many broken toys. There was a small depression in the ground near the center, filled with debris. Chris noticed small pools of water and mud collected in the depression. "Wonder if they're attracted to the water?"

The crying ceased abruptly, and the fireflies dispersed, their tiny lights dancing away to eventually encircle the farmhouse.

"That was weird... why did it stop?"

"Dunno," Chris replied, "and why are the lightning bugs up around the house now?"

"Something's happening up there?" Kat questioned in a puzzled voice.

"Maybe... let's go find out."

·»»—·•—·«·

"Norman, is anything happening on your cameras?" Chris's voice rattled in my ears and startled me awake. My heart raced as I sat up, disoriented in the darkened room. I had forgotten to remove the radio headset before falling asleep and could hear Norman's excited voice.

"We have movement!"

I heard the door swing open in the family room, followed by footsteps pounding on the wooden floor. I threw off my covers and ran into the room, still groggy from sleep. Chris and Kat were standing there, breathing heavily, staring at the Ovilus sitting on the floor. The temperature had dropped to a bitter cold, and I could see their breaths swirling in a fog around them.

"Wh-whats going on?" I stammered, rubbing my arms for warmth.

"We think Amelia might be trying to communicate with us." Chris replied.

The chilling air clung to my skin like icy tendrils, sending shivers through me. I listened intently as Chris asked Amelia questions, his voice soft and reassuring.

"Amelia, can you show yourself to us? We're not here to hurt you."

"AFRAID." a digital voice rang out as the Ovilus displayed the word.

"How old are you?"

Silence filled the room for a moment before the digitized voice replied once again.

"NINE."

"Did you live in this house?"

"YES." came the almost immediate reply, followed by two more words.

"ALLISON."

"MISS."

"Allison?" Kat mouthed the name and looked towards me

to see if I recognized it. I shrugged and shook my head, no.

"Where are your parents?" Chris continued, wanting Amelia to reveal more about herself.

The sensors on the device peaked and flashed wildly. Norman's voice crackled through the radio, informing us of a shadowy figure moving across his screen in the van.

"I think she's forming," he said, his voice tense with excitement. "I see a dark shadow moving around all of you."

"Can you give us a sign that you're with us, Amelia?" Chris asked, his eyes scanning the room. Suddenly, the television flickered to life, displaying an old TV show, '*Lawrence Laine's Starlight Review*.' The volume increased, growing steadily louder. Kat covered her ears and grimaced. A final flash of light blinded us before the screen faded to black, leaving us in darkness and silence.

"Norman, didn't you cut the power to the house earlier?" Chris asked over the headset, sounding a bit irritated. Norman confirmed that he had indeed turned off the power.

"Then how did the TV come on?" I asked as I watched Chris unplug the set. Kat, shaken by the sudden turn of events, mumbled something about needing the bathroom and hurried away.

"Was it Amelia?" I whispered, my breath visible in the frigid air. Was she... here?"

"Maybe," Chris replied, "Norman saw a shadow right before the TV - ."

"Guys, we have more activity!" Norman's voice crackled through the radio, interrupting our conversation. "Temperature readings are dropping in Maddie's bedroom."

My stomach twisted into knots at the mention of Maddie. I made a move to run to her room, but Chris caught my arm, stopping me in my tracks. "Wait," he said gently. "We need to make sure something's really happening."

"Is Maddie asleep, Norman?"

"Y-yes, she's still asleep," Norman confirmed after watching her on the monitor.

"Any visual signs of a presence?"

"Not at the moment," Norman replied.

"Alright, keep an eye on Maddie. We'll hang down here for now." Chris released my arm, but the concern in his eyes remained. I knew he could sense my fear for Maddie, but I had to trust in his ability to help her, and Amelia.

"Chris, the floor leading up the stairs is wet," Kat yelled out as she emerged from the bathroom, a hint of confusion in her voice.

Norman chimed in, "The firefly activity has increased outside the house, and several are landing on the windows of Maddie's room."

Chris and I both noticed the difference in our surroundings. The glow from the fireflies cast eerie patterns on the walls - a haunting dance of light and shadow. It felt as if we were trapped in some bizarre nightmare.

"Everyone be very still and stay where you are," Norman commanded over the headset. "I'm seeing a figure in Maddie's room. It looks... there's a little girl standing next to Maddie's bed. She just appeared out of thin air."

"Screw standing still!" Kat exclaimed, her brash personality refusing to be silenced even in this tense moment. "I wanna see this!" With a determined stride, she crept up the stairs and stopped near the top, peering cautiously into Maddie's room.

"Guys..." Kat's voice trailed off as she spoke into her headset. "You need to see this."

I steeled myself and ran through the kitchen to climb the stairs, Chris following close behind. Nearing the top, I grabbed Kat's arm.

"Is it Amelia?" I questioned in a quiet voice.

"It's her."

The scene unfolding before Kat's eyes was something she could never have imagined, even in her wildest dreams. She motioned for me to follow as she took the final few steps up and into the room.

"She's...talking to Maddie."

I quietly followed Kat into the room and saw Amelia's spirit. Her translucent form was rimmed by the flickering green light coming from the window. She leaned in close to Maddie, gently stroked her hair, and begin to whisper quietly. I could see her breath, a cold mist that hung in the air.

Chris moved up behind me so he could see. "Damn!" he muttered under his breath as the took in the scene unfolding before him.

"Look at that," Kat exhaled quietly, rubbing her cheeks to ward off the bitter chill that had filled the room. "There are thousands of them..."

I followed Kat's gaze to the window, now nearly opaque

with the mass of fireflies covering the glass.

"Amelia?" I called, as I stepped further in the room.

At the sound of my voice, Amelia turned, her eyes locking with mine. For a moment, we simply stared at one another, a gaze that was heavy with unspoken emotion. Then, ever so slowly, a smile crept across her tear-streaked face, a smile that held more pain than joy.

"What are you saying to her?" I asked, struggling to keep my voice steady.

Amelia didn't answer. Instead, she continued to smile through her tears, her gaze never leaving mine.

Kat broke the silence, cursing under her breath as she stared wide-eyed at the ghostly figure before us. "Jesus Christ," she exclaimed, the shock evident in her voice. "She's fricking real."

Suddenly, Amelia's expression changed. Her smile melted and her lips trembled as she began to cry. Her sobs filled the room, echoing through the cold air and tugging at my heartstrings. The lights outside the window glowed brighter, illuminating her tear-stained face.

"Please," I pleaded, desperation seeping into my tone. "Tell us what you want. Help us understand."

Amelia raised her hand a pointed towards the window, her gaze locked on something beyond it we couldn't see. Without warning, she vanished in a wispy trail of smoke and shadow, leaving behind a faint echo of crying, and the cold chill of her presence.

The room fell silent, the weight of what we'd just witnessed settling over us like a shroud. I felt a strange mix of relief and dread wash over me.

"Guys! She's gone, but I got it all! Recorded everything!" Norman's voice crackled through our headsets. "I'm coming inside!"

"Turn the power back on before you come in," Chris barked, "We need some light in here."

"Okay," Norman answered, his voice filled with excitement.

The eerie green glow had vanished from the windows, replaced by the familiar darkness of night. I flicked on the bedside lamp and waited for the power to come back on. Within seconds a warm yellow light filled the room.

"Hey Sam, I gotta hit the bathroom again," Kat mumbled, looking uncomfortable as she crossed one leg over the other in a weird little dance. I nodded and turned my attention to Maddie. Her hair and nightgown were damp and cold, clinging to her small form. I felt a shiver run through me as I noticed the faint rasp that accompanied each labored breath.

"Maddie, you okay?" I asked gently, shaking her awake. She stirred, her eyes fluttering open to meet mine.

"I'm cold," she whispered, her voice weak and airy. "And my legs hurt so bad." My heart ached at the sight of her trembling lips, and I immediately pulled her close, trying to share my warmth.

"Shh, it's okay," I murmured, rubbing her back as she started to cry. Driven by concern, I pulled the covers back to examine her body, and gasped in horror at the sight of bruised, scraped, and bloody legs.

"Chris!" I cried out, my hands shaking as I tried to process the extent of Maddie's injuries. He rushed to my side, shocked by the wounds on Maddie's legs.

"Sam, we need to clean her up," he said urgently. "Got any bandages or a first-aid kit I can use?"

"Downstairs bathroom," I choked out, pointing towards the stairs. I noticed water on the floor, accompanied by dirty little footprints that could only have been made by a child.

Chris sprinted down the stairs. At the bottom, he nearly collided with Kat, who was clutching her stomach. "You look like you've seen a ghost," he said, slightly exasperated.

"Ha! Funny!" she replied sarcastically, rolling her eyes. Norman joined them, excitedly chattering about the events and all the data he had recorded. Chris pushed past both, grabbed the first-aid kit from the bathroom, and raced back upstairs.

"Normie, your data ain't nonthin' like what I saw up there," Kat taunted him as they followed Chris.

With every gentle dab of the cotton swab, I could see Maddie wincing in pain. Chris worked meticulously to clean her wounds, and I couldn't help but feel a pang of guilt for not being able to protect her from this. He finished bandaging her scraped legs, and I lifted her gently into my arms.

"Come on, sweetie, let's get you to my bed." I was determined to keep Maddie close to me for the remainder of the night. Chris followed me down the stairs, holding an arm to help steady me as I walked. His presence behind me was comforting.

"Stay with her," he instructed me softly as I laid Maddie on my bed. "I'll be nearby if you need anything." He then motioned for Kat and Norman to follow him outside.

Chris wasted no time getting to the point as they climbed into the back of the van. "Norman, have you come across anything like this in your research, where someone has been physically harmed by a spirit?"

Norman adjusted his glasses, searching his memory. "Well, there's no scientific evidence to support claims of harm caused by entities. Most of the evidence is based on anecdotal accounts and personal beliefs rather than empirical data. It's important to note that the idea of ghosts causing harm is primarily rooted in folklore, mythology, and popular culture."

"However," he continued, "there have been accounts of malevolent spirits or ghosts that cause harm to humans."

"Amelia didn't seem mean, though," Kat interjected, her voice surprisingly soft. "I mean, when I made eye contact with her... it felt like she was just... sad, and I never saw her touch Maddie's legs."

"Regardless," Chris said firmly, "we need to figure out what's going on here and how to protect Maddie. Norman, can you replay the video from Maddie's room?" Chris asked, his voice tense.

"Sure thing," Norman replied, fiddling with some buttons. "You won't believe the evidence we've got!" His voice was slightly shrill and excited. "This is some next-level stuff!"

"Screw your evidence, Normie," Kat scoffed, rolling her eyes. "I was there. I don't need your 'evidence' to know what went down."

"Guys, not now," Chris snapped. "Just show the

playback."

The three of them huddled together in the van, the video screen casting an eerie glow on their faces. Chris watched as Amelia appeared beside Maddie's bed, her ghostly form outlined by the glowing insects landing on the window. He could hear Maddie's raspy breathing grow heavier as Amelia touched her. Amelia's crying echoed through the speakers, filling the van with a haunting sadness.

As the recording reached its climax, Amelia vanished, leaving only the sound of her crying behind. Norman stopped the playback, but her sobs continued, seemingly louder than before.

"Norman, stop the playback," Chris snapped, irritation creeping into his voice.

"I did," Norman replied, his eyes wide with surprise. "That crying isn't coming from the video."

"Then where is it coming from?" Chris asked, his mind racing.

"Outside," Kat whispered, her voice trembling with excitement.

They exchanged knowing glances before leaping out of the van. The faint sound of crying grew louder as they walked into the pasture behind the barn. The first rays of daylight appeared on the horizon, beyond the thousands of fireflies that swirled above a single point in the field.

"Whatever's happening here," Chris said, his voice low and urgent, "this is unlike anything we've ever dealt with before."

"Agreed," Norman added, his scientific mind taking over. "Wait 'till we show this footage to the world. We'll be on

CNN, YouTube, everywhere!" he blabbered excitedly. "No way anyone can debunk this!"

"Nobody's going to see anything," Chris responded, tempering Norman's enthusiasm. "We need to figure this out ourselves before letting anyone else in on it. Besides, Samantha and Maddie don't need crowds of people tramping around here asking questions."

"Chris is a hundred percent right." Kat agreed and pointed her finger accusingly at Norman. "Keep this between us, or else..." Her voice trailed away in a veiled but unspoken threat.

"Let's wrap things up for the night and get some rest," Chris concluded. "We need to prepare ourselves for an extended stay."

"This ain't yo mama's ghost tour!" Kat drawled, slapping Norman on his back. Norman recoiled, raising his fist in mock outrage at Kat as she stuck out her tongue and darted away.

"Kat's got a point," Chris mused to himself, watching Norman angrily chase Kat back to the van. "We've got a real spirit to deal with here."

Chapter Seven

Lawrence Laine's Starlight Review

New York City, 1951

The clock ticked away, its hands inching closer to the top of the hour. The atmosphere backstage at the CBN Studios Theater was a whirlwind of activity, as performers and crew members scurried about in preparation for the televised performance of "Lawrence Laine's Starlight Revue."

"Alright, everyone! Make final preparations to go live!" shouted an assistant stage manager, clipboard clutched tightly in his hand as he hurriedly checked off items on his list. In the dimly lit backstage, the cacophony of performers rehearsing seemed to echo off the walls like a haunting melody. A violinist meticulously tuned her instrument, her fingers deftly adjusting the tension of the strings. Nearby, a group of dancers practiced their intricate steps, their fluid movements a mesmerizing dance of shadows against the backdrop. In a corner, a magician inspected his deck of cards with a critical eye, ensuring each card was in perfect order for his upcoming illusion.

The Green Room was awash in a warm glow of camaraderie, as performers took respite from the chaos outside, sipping cocktails and nibbling on hors d'oeuvres. Laughter rang out as they exchanged stories, seeking solace in the familiarity of shared experiences. Some of the more well-known performers ventured out into the studio audience, signing autographs and posing for photographs with eager fans. The crowd buzzed with excitement, each interaction with their idols adding to the anticipation of the live performance.

"All performers, listen up!" boomed a voice, cutting through the chatter and commotion. The stage manager stood tall, his gaze sweeping across the bustling scene backstage, demanding attention. "We have one hour until we go live! Please take your assigned places backstage or in your dressing room!"

A ripple of excitement surged through the performers, propelling them into action.

"Watch your step," cautioned a prop master as he carefully navigated his way through the bustling space, arms laden with props, costumes, and various other items necessary for the acts that would soon grace the stage.

"Is this really necessary?" asked a dancer, eyeing the assortment of props placed around her as she practiced her routine. Her movements were fluid and graceful, like a swan gliding through water. She adjusted her steps, ensuring she wouldn't stumble.

"Of course, it is," replied the prop master with a hint of sarcasm. "This is Lawrence Laine's show. Everything has to be perfect."

The mention of Lawrence Laine's name seemed to hang in the air like an invisible weight, reminding everyone present of the high stakes of this performance.

Laine had been a well-known radio performer before his transition to the world of television. He was renowned for his outgoing personality and ostentatious lifestyle, which added to his status as a true celebrity.

The stage itself was a masterpiece of elegance; the opulent backdrop glistened under the warm glow of the overhead lights, while elaborate curtains framed the scene with a rich, velvety texture. The design was nothing short of breathtaking, and it was clear that great care had been taken to ensure this night would be one for the ages. Lighting technicians climbed their ladders and adjusted the incandescent lights and spotlights.

"I need more light on center stage!" barked the lead technician, a wiry man in his forties whose eye was as sharp as an eagle's. "We want our performers to shine, not disappear into the background."

The stage came alive under the expert hands of the technicians, and the theater itself seemed to grow more vibrant, suffused with the energy of countless sponsors whose banners and advertisements adorned every available surface. An almost tangible tension filled the room - an atmosphere that crackled with electricity and an expectation that anything could happen when the curtains rose.

Lawrence Laine gazed into the mirror in his private dressing room; his salt-and-pepper locks carefully styled, a glass of bourbon held within one of his hands and a lit cigarette dangling from the other. In his tailored tuxedo, Lawrence was every inch the charismatic star he had built his career on being - a man who could captivate an audience and command a room with just a smile.

"Lawrence, you're playing with fire!" George's voice thundered from behind him, carrying a mixture of frustration and concern. George Benningly had been Lawrence's friend and confidant for as long as either of them could remember, and he was usually the first choice when there were matters that required a discreet touch. Dressed in a sharp gray suit, George paced across the cramped space, hands clenched. "Your ratings are plummeting, and you're willing to risk everything for this? If your sponsors get wind of it, they'll be gone... done."

Allison Luce, Lawrence's young and alluring assistant, sat nervously on the vanity chair. Her red lipstick shimmered beneath the soft glow of the dressing room lights, her auburn curls cascading down her shoulders. Her fingers toyed nervously with the pearls around her neck, betraying the fear she tried so hard to hide.

"George," Lawrence murmured, a wry smile tugging at the corners of his mouth, "you'll take care of this for me, won't you?"

"I can only do so much!" George's voice rose in pitch as his frustration peaked.

Lawrence took a swig of bourbon, his eyes never leaving Allison's reflection in the mirror before him. He took a long drag on his cigarette and exhaled a cloud of smoke; his voice was raspy but filled the room easily as he spoke. "Allison, you're my everything. We won't let anything get between us."

She hesitated, her green eyes searching his face for reassurance. "I know, Lawrence, but—"

"But she's pregnant," George blurted out, cutting her off before she could finish her sentence. "Lawrence, it's not just your career at stake here. It's your family, your reputation. You've got people who admire you, and you don't want to end up as tabloid gossip."

A flicker of doubt clouded Lawrence's eyes for a moment, but he quickly masked it with another sip of bourbon. "Let them gossip," he said, the liquid courage fortifying his resolve. "It's just part of the game."

"I'm scared," Allison spoke up, her voice trembling with emotion. He turned to her, his gaze softening as it met hers. The hint of vulnerability in her eyes tugged at something deep within him, making his heart race faster than any applause ever could.

"Come on, Lawrence, seriously, you've gotta get it together!" George snapped, his fancy shoes clacking loudly in the tiny room as he paced around. He could tell his friend was about to lose it, going all-in on this girl and risking everything.

Unfazed, Lawrence flicked his cigarette into a nearby ashtray and chuckled, a mischievous glint in his eye. "Relax, man. Everything's gonna be fine... you'll make sure it is."

A tense silence filled the room, interrupted only by the noise of performers shuffling around outside the dressing room door. Lawrence knew that George was right, that his actions had consequences that reached far beyond his own life. But the thought of losing Allison, of giving up what they had together, was intolerable.

"George," Lawrence spoke gently, his eyes going back to his friend, "you've had my back when things got rough. I'm counting on you to help us through this."

Lawrence took another drag of his cigarette, the tendrils of smoke curling into the dimly lit dressing room like ghostly fingers, a stark reminder of the dilemma that haunted the three people within it. His lips curled into a smirk. "That's why I love you. You'll come up with some arrangement that'll keep this all under wraps... our little secret."

The mirror caught the dark circles under Lawrence's eyes, a testament to the stress he'd been under lately. He placed his glass on the table with a deliberate clink and moved closer to Allison, his hand reaching out to caress her cheek.

George shook his head, his annoyance boiling over like a pot left on a stove too long. "You're not seeing it, are you? The competition's tough out there. 'The Milton Variety Hour' is getting popular, and 'The Sullivan Show' is right behind you in the ratings. We can't handle any more scandals, seriously."

Lawrence looked away from Allison, his sly grin reflecting in the mirror as he met George's gaze. "Speaking of Milton, did you hear they're having sponsor trouble? Seems like they can't keep up with my charm."

George sighed and rubbed his temples to ease his frustration. "Come on, man, this isn't a joke," he said, looking at Lawrence, who seemed completely unyielding.

It was like trying to talk to a brick wall.

Lawrence's eyes were full of longing as he leaned in for a passionate kiss with Allison. Just when their lips were about to touch, a sudden knock on the door startled them both.

"Five minutes to air, Mr. Laine!" the stage manager called out.

"Go on, babe," Lawrence whispered into Allison's ear, his voice husky and low. "Head up to the control room and enjoy the show." With one last lingering look, Allison whispered, "I love you," before slipping out of the dressing room, leaving behind only the faintest trace of her perfume.

As George seethed, Lawrence studied his friend's reflection in the mirror, mentally calculating his next move. He knew he was playing a dangerous game, but the thrill of it all made him feel alive. The stakes were high, and he reveled in the feeling of dancing on the edge.

"You've changed," George said, taking a step closer, his voice low and angry. "You used to have some morals, and you cared about your work. Now it's all about who you can bed next." George shook his head and seemed genuinely sad. "You've screwed yourself this time, buddy. There's a kid on the way."

Lawrence studied George for a moment, his mood shifting. "You might be right. Maybe I am screwed, maybe not. I guess time will tell."

A knock on the door brought them both back to reality as a stage manager called out from the other side, "One minute to air. We need you in place, Mr. Laine." Lawrence straightened his tie and put out his cigarette, the smoke curling up towards the ceiling as his eyes locked onto George's.

"You know that old farmhouse on my estate, the one by the road?" George nodded, recalling the small, aged building on the edge of the sprawling Laine property.

"See that Allison is comfortable there. You'll do that for me, won't you, George?" Lawrence's voice held a note of pleading, the first time George had heard it in years. He reluctantly nodded in agreement, knowing that he was once again being drawn into fixing another of his best friend's scandals.

The sound of the audience cheering and the orchestra playing the 'Starlight Revue Theme' echoed into the dressing room as Lawrence headed towards the door. "Showtime!" he exclaimed, a wide grin plastered across his face as he patted George on the back and walked out the door, leaving him to contemplate what needed to be done. The weight of the task ahead settled heavily on his shoulders as he stared at the now-empty dressing room, the shadows of secrets and lies closing in around him.

Chapter Eight

Isn't It Strange?

The small, cramped office in Leesburg buzzed with an air of tension as Chris paced back and forth, phone pressed to his ear. Papers were strewn across the desk, evidence of the long hours spent researching and preparing for the team's next move. The dim light from the solitary desk lamp cast shadows on the walls, adding to the atmosphere of mystery that enveloped the room.

"Sam, how's Maddie holding up after last night?" Chris asked, concern etched into his furrowed brow.

"I don't think you'll believe me if I tell you," Samantha replied, her voice carrying a hint of disbelief. "Her cuts are barely visible today... it's like they just went away. I can see some marks, but no wounds like last night."

Chris stopped pacing, his eyes widened in surprise. "That's...unexpected. I thought those scrapes were pretty deep." Chris rubbed the back of his neck to relieve the tightness that came with his anxiety. "I hate to admit it, but I feel a bit out of my league here. We need to be more cautious going forward."

"It's unnerving to say the least, but I'm not taking any

chances. If Amelia even gives a hint that she's about to make an appearance, we're out of here." Sam assured him.

"Call me if anything happens," Chris quickly responded. "You can always bring Maddie here to the office."

"Thanks, Chris. I'll do that."

"Good," Chris nodded, remembering the harrowing experience. "I'm really sorry that happened to Maddie last night. You know I'd never do anything to put you or her in harm's way."

"I know... none of us knew anything like that was going to happen." Sam took a deep breath before finishing her thought. "Now we know."

"I sent Kat and Norman to do some research, property records, newspaper articles... anything that could help us learn more about Amelia and her story. We need to put her to rest, and any clues we uncover could help. Giving her peace... that should end the activity."

"God, I hope you're right," Sam replied, her voice wavering slightly, betraying her fear. "I just want all of this to be over and for Maddie to be safe."

"Me too, Sam," Chris said softly, his voice filled with compassion. "We're all planning on being back at the farmhouse tonight if that's ok with you. We're not going to conduct another investigation, but we'll be there, set up and ready in case anything happens."

"Thanks, Chris," Samantha whispered, her gratitude evident in her voice. "I'll see you later then."

"See you soon." Chris ended the call and stared at the now silent phone, his mind racing.

The door to the cramped office creaked open, and

Norman stepped in clutching a worn manila folder. He looked slightly disheveled, his tie crooked and hair mussed, as if he'd been rifling through a dusty closet all day.

"I think I've found something," Norman announced.

"Alright, what've you got?" Chris asked, sitting on the edge of his desk, and gesturing for Norman to take a seat across from him.

Norman sat in his desk chair and eagerly flipped open the folder, pulling out a group of documents. "I've been researching the property records for the farmhouse like you asked. Check this out." He pointed to one document. "It shows that in 1951, the property was divided and transferred from the Lawrence Laine estate to George Benningly."

"George Benningly," Chris mumbled under his breath, "Who was that, exactly?"

"From what I've read he was Laine's best friend... worked with him on the show."

Chris glanced away from the map and stared blankly into space. "I've definitely heard that name before, but I just can't remember why."

"Same here," Norman admitted.

"Maybe it'll come to us," Chris suggested, turning back to scan the rest of the documents. "What's this?"

"It's a map of the Laine estate." Norman stood and unfolded a large, yellowed map onto Chris's desk, revealing an extensive property that sprawled over 1,900 acres. Chris whistled in amazement.

"Look here," Norman pointed to a small square niche cut

into the southernmost boundary of the property. "This is the plot acquired by Benningly. It's where the farmhouse currently stands."

"So, for some reason, Laine decided to give or sell this little piece of land to Benningly...why?"

"Don't know," Norman shrugged and straightened his glasses. "Maybe to settle a debt or reward him for some reason? It wasn't for money. Laine didn't need money."

"I would think giving money would be a nice reward for anyone - friend or not. Transferring this property to Benningly- this was something more. Laine wanted to give something personal to Benningly."

"Maybe a reward for loyalty?" Norman questioned, equally curious about the transaction.

"Maybe," Chris mused, his eyes narrowing as he studied the map further. "So, what happened to the rest of Laine's estate?"

"Sold off to a Saudi prince in the late 1970s," Norman replied, flipping to another map that showed just the smaller property. "But look at this - there was originally an earlier house that was destroyed or torn down. A new structure was built on the same site in the early 1920s."

"That explains the stone foundation we saw in the basement," Chris nodded knowingly. "The house built in the 20's, that's the farmhouse we have today?"

"Same as today, although there were modifications and additions built in later years." Norman traced his finger along the map, indicating several smaller buildings and a well.

"A well?" Chris looked closer at the mark on the map.

"Ok, so that's..." Chris's voice trailed off as he realized the significance of the mark. "That's the exact spot where we saw all the fireflies last night."

"They were swarming over the well!" Norman exclaimed, his eyes lighting up. "There must be something about that location that attracts them... and the crying we heard."

"Amelia's crying," Chris answered, remembering the chilling sobs he had heard from Amelia's spirit form.

"Maybe the fireflies are attracted to Amelia's spirit," Norman mumbled as he rubbed his chin. "I mean, scientifically it could be an energy field they're drawn to."

"Or water... I saw water on the ground around the stones last night."

"True, could be water," Norman nodded in agreement, "but what about the crying?"

Chris thought for a moment, weighing the spiritual and scientific evidence they'd witnessed before drawing a conclusion. "I think Amelia's spirit is drawn to this well for some reason," Chris said, his voice heavy and convincing. "We need some answers before Amelia pays another visit to Maddie. She can't go through another night like last night."

"Agreed," Norman nodded solemnly. "That was brutal... why do you think Amelia did that to Maddie?"

"I'm not sure she did it on purpose... maybe she was just wanting Maddie to feel what she was feeling, and it manifest itself as injuries."

Chris glanced up at Norman and gave a small, helpless shrug, unsure of his hunch.

"It's strange that they have that connection. Why do you

think Amelia is attracted to Maddie?" Norman countered, equally baffled.

"Not sure... maybe it's their ages... they seem to be about the same age. Maybe it's emotional - something connected to Maddie's illness."

"Maddie's sick?" Norman questioned, looking genuinely surprised.

"She's terminally ill." Chris locked eyes with Norman as he spoke. "That's why Sam brought her to the farmhouse - to spend time with her before she passes."

Norman settled back into his chair, obviously stunned by Chris's words. He stared blankly ahead as his thoughts consumed him. "I... I didn't know, but it does explain a possible spiritual connection on an emotional level, some shared fear."

"Or pain," Chris added solemnly. "Maybe Maddie's wounds were Amelia's way of showing her the pain she's experiencing."

The shrill ring of Chris' cell phone broke the tense silence in the cramped office, causing Norman to jump. Chris quickly grabbed his phone and saw Kat's name flashing on the screen.

"Hey, Kat," he answered, putting her on speakerphone so that Norman could join in on the conversation. "What's up?"

"I've got the scoop on Amelia!" Kat exclaimed triumphantly from her end of the line. The echoey background suggested that she was still at the Thomas Balch Library in downtown Leesburg. "I found some newspaper articles on microfiche about her disappearance. You want me to read 'em to you?"

"Absolutely." Chris glanced over at Norman, who looked equally eager to hear what Kat had discovered. "You're on speaker, by the way. Say hi to Norman."

"Hey, Normie," Kat teased, her voice dripping with sarcasm. "Got any grey hairs sprouting in your pubes after last night? That was some scary shit, huh. Oh wait... do you even have pubes yet?"

"Can the insults, Kat," Norman snapped, clearly unamused by her jest. "And yes, I have pubes. At least I don't need diapers when I get spooked like you do."

"Just read the article you found," Chris interrupted loudly, raising an eyebrow at Norman.

"Articles, actually," Kat corrected Chris, the sound of shuffling in the background. "Hang on, I'm trying to get this ancient machine to cooperate.

Shit... damn it!" she muttered under her breath as she wrestled to load the bulky microfiche reader.

"Got it!" she announced, finally. In the dimly lit room, she squinted at the tiny thumbnail-sized images, adjusting the focus until the first article came into view.

"Okay, so this first one is about Amelia's disappearance. It's from the Leesburg Gazette and it's dated July 6, 1961." She began reading aloud, her voice taking on a somber tone.

```
Headline: Mysterious Disappearance
         Shrouds Old Waterford Road Farmhouse
```

> Byline: Martha Thompson, Leesburg
> Gazette, July 6, 1961
>
> LEESBURG, Virginia — A cloud
> of mystery surrounds the quiet
> countryside as Allison Luce, a young
> woman in her late 20s, and her
> daughter, Amelia, aged 9, have gone
> missing from their rural farmhouse on
> Old Waterford Road.

"We have a last name now," Chris interrupted. "Luce... that could be helpful."

"Yup," Kat responded and continued to read.

> The disappearance came to light when
> local authorities were alerted by
> an anonymous source who claimed the
> family was unresponsive to repeated
> attempts at communication.

"Why anonymous?" Norman interjected, "Why keep your name a secret when you're trying to check up on someone?"

"Maybe so you won't be involved if something ends up not being okay." Chris responded.

Kat sighed, upset by the constant interruptions. "Are you guys going to listen or what?"

"Go on, Kat." Chris held a finger to his lips motioning for

Norman to be silent.

> Leesburg Police, acting on the tip, visited the residence only to find it eerily vacant. There were no apparent signs of struggle, and the personal belongings of the mother and daughter remained undisturbed, leading investigators to believe they may have left in haste. The absence of any clear motive or clue has left both investigators and the community puzzled, with speculations circulating about the circumstances of their sudden departure. Volunteers from the local community have rallied to conduct a thorough search of the surrounding area in hopes of shedding light on the mysterious disappearance. The Leesburg Police Department is urging anyone with information regarding the whereabouts of Allison and Amelia to come forward.

Chris and Norman exchanged grim glances. "So, we can assume this is 'our' Amelia, and she and her mom just disappeared one day," Chris spoke as he stood and paced the room. "Any idea as to what happened to them?"

"Keep listening," Kat urged. "I've got a follow-up article

here." She fumbled with another card as she loaded the microfiche reader.

"Let me just get this thing loaded... Okay... got it. Here's a follow-up article dated July 20, 1961."

Headline: **Search for Missing Leesburg Family Comes to an End**

Byline: Robert Reynolds, Leesburg Gazette, July 20, 1961

LEESBURG, Virginia — The exhaustive two-week search for Allison and Amelia Luce, who mysteriously vanished from their rural farmhouse outside Leesburg, has concluded with no signs of the missing family. Despite the determined efforts of local authorities and volunteers, the operation is regrettably being called off, as it has yielded no substantial leads or evidence to unravel the mystery surrounding their disappearance. The absence of any tangible clues has left both investigators and the community at large perplexed. The abrupt and unexplained nature of their vanishing has left a tangible sense of unease among neighbors and friends. As the search concludes, local authorities vow to keep the case open, underscoring the importance of community cooperation. Residents are urged to come forward with any information that may shed light on the whereabouts of Allison and Amelia Luce.

"Isn't it strange," Norman interjected, his voice tight with unease, "that they never found anything at all? It's like they just vanished into thin air." He paused, contemplating the thought. "Could they have been kidnapped?"

Chris considered this possibility. "Maybe," he conceded, "but the articles don't mention anything about a kidnapping or ransom. I'm sure they would have looked into that aspect... and they ended the search a couple of weeks after she went missing claiming they had no evidence or leads."

"We've seen Amelia's spirit," Norman added, "so she must've died at some point, either at the time of her disappearance or shortly after."

"She's definitely dead!" Kat chimed in, her voice taking on a more animated tone. "And judging by the spook I saw; she was around nine years old when she died."

Norman couldn't resist taking a jab at Kat's enthusiasm. "Well, I think we all could see the apparition was a little girl, Kat. Not exactly a revelation," he said sarcastically, a thin smile crossing his lips.

"Okay, smart ass, you want a revelation?" Kat shot back defiantly, her voice crackling with energy over the phone. "Listen to this." There was a clanking of machinery and a few more expletives before she began to read the final newspaper article, dated a month after the search for Amelia had been called off.

Headline: **Local Authorities Shift Focus, Deem Luce Family Disappearance Suspicious**

Byline: Evelyn Turner, Leesburg Gazette, August 17, 1961

LEESBURG, Virginia — In a significant development, local law enforcement has shifted gears in the investigation into the disappearance of Allison and Amelia Luce. After uncovering prior connections between the Luce family and another local resident, authorities are now treating the case as suspicious, with the unsettling possibility of foul play. The investigation remains ongoing, with law enforcement

> *conducting interviews. The decision to label the disappearance as suspicious marks a pivotal turn in the case, raising questions and concerns among the Leesburg community. Details surrounding the connections and potential motives are not being released. Further details are pending.*

"Damn," Chris muttered, letting out a low whistle. "That puts a new spin on things."

"Indeed," Norman agreed. "This could confirm our thoughts about more sinister things happening here."

"True," Chris nodded, rubbing his chin thoughtfully. "But part of me wonders if Allison and Amelia just took off."

"Wouldn't they pack up their stuff and take it with 'em, though?" Kat asked pointedly.

"Usually, that would be the case," Chris agreed. "Unless there was some urgent reason for them to leave. Nevertheless, we need more details about Allison Luce. There must be something about her that can provide insight into what happened."

"I've got one more tidbit about Allison and Amelia to add to the riddle." As if on cue, Kat's voice thundered through the speakerphone, a slight crackle interspersed among her words.

"Saving the best for last I hope," Chris urged, leaning

forward in his chair. "What is it?"

"Turns out I found Amelia's birth certificate over in the library's genealogical center." Chris's eyes narrowed as he listened intently. "Amelia Luce was born on February 14th, 1952, to Allison Luce."

"Valentine's Day," Norman murmured under his breath, considering the significance of the date.

"Yep," Kat continued, "and get this, she was born in the farmhouse, not in a hospital... the address is listed and it's our farmhouse. The birth was attended by a midwife named Alba Weston."

"That confirms it... it's our Amelia," Chris murmured, stroking his chin as the pieces of the puzzle slowly began to fit together. "And what about Amelia's father?"

"Ah, that's the thing," Kat replied with a sly chuckle. "There's no name given for the father on the birth certificate."

"Of course not," Norman muttered under his breath.

"Looks like the plot thickens," Chris remarked, a hint of a smile tugging at the corners of his mouth. "Good job finding that information, Kat. Make sure to get copies of the birth certificate and newspaper articles, then join us back here at the office."

"Already have the copies," she replied, her tone cocky and confident. "Hey, are we heading back to the farmhouse tonight?"

"Yep," Chris confirmed, already considering the logistics for their return. "Pack some sleeping bags and any other essentials you might need for another overnight stay."

"Great... another sleepless night!" Kat said, about to hang

up when Norman chimed in.

"Hey, don't forget your makeup bag, Skittles!" he teased. "And maybe you should pack a couple of diapers as well."

"Norman, goddamit I swear—" Kat began, her voice rising in protest.

"Talk soon," Chris cut in, ending the speakerphone call, and sparing them both from a heated exchange.

Chris leaned against the edge of his cluttered desk, watching as Norman paced in front of the window; a newly formed rain shower streaked the glass casting a somber mood over the cramped office. The air felt heavy with unspoken questions.

"Norman, what are your thoughts on all this?" Chris asked, breaking the silence.

"I don't know," he finally admitted. "There's just something about all this that's... it's unsettling."

Norman stopped pacing and stared out at the downpour. "I think it's all connected to the property," he began slowly, turning to face Chris. "Maybe that's why the TV magically keeps playing the old *'Starlight Review'* show... perhaps Amelia wants us to know Laine is involved somehow."

"Go on," Chris urged, sensing Norman might be on to something.

"Amelia was born in the farmhouse, so she and Allison had to have lived there for at least 9 years, because the newspaper articles said Amelia was 9 when they went missing," Norman explained, his expression serious. "But Allison's name isn't on any of the property records, so why is that?" Norman took a few strides closer to the window and gazed outside at the rain. "The only facts connecting

Laine to any of this is the transfer of the property to Benningly. How could he be connected to Allis..." Norman stopped mid-sentence, his words caught in his throat. "Do you think Lawrence Laine was involved with Allison... like an affair?" Norman's eyes widened at the possibility.

"Could be," Chris agreed, sounding surprised. "It would explain why Allison was staying at the farmhouse, and why she kept Amelia's paternity a secret."

"Wow," Norman breathed, his eyes wide with shock. "If Laine is Amelia's father, that's... that's huge. If it's true, then this whole thing just got a lot more complicated."

"It did." Chris replied, his voice firm yet tinged with uncertainty. "It's a wild theory, but it might just be the key to understanding what happened to Amelia and Allison."

Norman nodded and leaned against the window, letting the possible consequences of this theory sink in. "We'll have to tread carefully moving forward."

Chris sat at his desk, his fingers drumming its surface in a rhythmic cadence that signified he was deep in thought.

"Chris," Norman turned to face his friend, "it's an interesting mix of facts and paranormal observations that we've gathered so far. But we can't ignore either side."

"True," Chris agreed, "But we have to examine the spiritual and factual aspects separately before drawing any conclusions. Each has its own unique set of circumstances that we need.to consider."

"Fair enough." Norman conceded, adjusting his glasses. "But our investigation at the farmhouse did lead us to the facts we uncovered today. In a way, the spiritual revealed the factual."

"Can't argue with you there, Norman." Chris stood up from his chair and paced the room, his brow furrowed. "We need to be prepared for our next encounter with Amelia. The facts point to a possible sinister cause for her demise... police suspected foul play. If that manifests itself in a spiritual way it could have a significant impact on Maddie."

"Agreed," Norman replied, nodding solemnly. "But how do we prepare ourselves for something like that?"

"Knowledge is power, my friend," Chris said, a determined glint in his eyes. "We need to find out more about everyone involved."

Norman nodded in agreement. "Maybe I should contact George over at the Loudoun County Historical Society. He probably knows a lot about Laine."

"George?"

Chris gave Norman a questioning glance before turning to the bookcase behind his desk. He rummaged through the shelves until he located a Civil War History book published by the local society, and quickly flipped through the pages to reveal the name of its executive director, George Benningly, Jr.

"Now I remember why the name sounded so familiar. George Benningly is the executive director of the Loudoun County Historical Society."

"Holy shit, you're right! George's last name is... wait..." Norman's words slowly died away as he contemplated the figures in his head. "It can't be the same George Benningly. The property transfer was dated 1951. Anyone alive then would be in their late 90's at least - or dead by now."

"George junior." Chris replied, reading the name in the book again. "I think they're related, but there's only one way to find out... I need to pay a visit to Mr. Benningly. I'll give him a call and set up an appointment for tomorrow. He always likes giving me a hard time about my job... makes for good conversation."

"Yeah, history guys don't dig ghost hunters," Norman chuckled.

Chapter Nine

Shadows In the Trees

Chris pulled up to the van at the farmhouse, his eyes immediately drawn to Norman's old Opal GT parked nearby. Leaning against the van was a black Coleman scooter, Kat's main source of transportation. "Looks like the gang's all here," he muttered under his breath as he parked and exited the truck.

"Chris!" Kat yelled as she walked hand in hand with Maddie. "We're heading to the barn to check out Amelia's toys before it gets dark. Maddie wants to show me the book Amelia was reading."

"Sounds like a plan," Chris replied, trying to sound relaxed despite an underlying concern. "Just stay on your toes and be careful, alright? And Kat... any sign of Amelia, get out right away."

Kat rolled her eyes in her usual cocky manner but nodded in agreement. "I'm not sticking around if any spooks make an appearance," she chuckled. "Been there, done that."

Chris watched them walk away, his heart warmed by the connection forming between Maddie and Kat. He couldn't help but feel that the ghostly encounters had made them *all* closer.

Norman was busy adjusting various knobs on equipment inside the van, fine-tuning the devices for the evening's observations. The tall, lanky nerd seemed completely oblivious to Chris's presence.

"Hey, Norman, did Kat leave those copies she made at the library with you?"

Without looking up, Norman handed Chris a folder stuffed with papers. "That's what she left in here," he replied, slightly miffed at the interruption. "I assume it's all there, but I haven't had a chance to look through it."

"No worries," Chris said, taking the folder from him. "I'll go over it with Sam. Have you seen her around?"

Norman finally glanced up to make eye contact with Chris. "Last time I saw her, she was on the front porch."

"Thanks, Norm." With that, Chris turned and headed for the front of the farmhouse, folder in hand.

I huddled in the rocker, my blanket drawn tight around me to ward off the cool night air. My body ached from exhaustion, and my thoughts were consumed with worry for Maddie.

"Samantha," Chris called out softly as he approached the porch steps, drawing my attention. "How are you holding up?"

"Been better," I admitted, offering him a weak smile. "I

haven't had much sleep since last night. Kat told me you guys did some research today. Find anything useful?"

"Maybe," he replied, holding up the folder. "Mind if I join you?"

"Been saving a spot for you...have a seat."

Chris settled down next to me, the warmth of his body comforting in the chilly evening air. We sat in silence for a moment, both of us watching the sun dip low on the horizon.

"Beautiful, isn't it?" Chris remarked, his voice barely above a whisper. "The way the sky fades from gold to pink and then to purple... It's like a painting."

"Yeah," I agreed, feeling my heart flutter at his poetic words. "It really is."

"I was thinking," he began hesitantly, "how 'bout we take a little walk. The rain's passed, and it really is nice out. We can walk and talk about the info we came up with today."

"What about Maddie?" I asked, reluctant to leave her alone even for a few minutes.

"Kats with her," Chris assured me. "They're checking out Amelia's things in the barn, and besides, we can make our walk a short one. I think it'll do you some good to get out and stretch your legs."

"Maybe so," I agreed, taking a deep breath of the fresh, post-rain air. "I think a walk would be good."

Chris and I strolled past the van, waving to Norman who was still tinkering with equipment. We exited the gate onto 'Old Waterford Road', heading down the tree-covered roadway as it gently sloped away from the farmhouse. Colorful leaves dotted the ground around us, and we carefully stepped around puddles left from the earlier rain.

"Looks like the lightning bugs are eager for nighttime," Chris said with a smile, his eyes following one of the tiny insects as it danced through the air.

"Seems that way," I replied, my gaze also tracking the firefly's path. "They're quite beautiful, aren't they?"

"Interesting insects for sure." Chris paused for a moment before continuing. "So, how's Maddie feeling? She looked pretty happy when she was with Kat."

"She's good, considering everything that's happened," I answered, my thoughts turning to the previous night's events. "She doesn't seem the least bit afraid of Amelia. In fact, she talks about her constantly."

"Maybe she doesn't feel threatened. Kids see things their own way I guess," Chris said thoughtfully. "How are you holding up... mentally I mean?"

I hesitated, unsure how honest I should be. "I'm doing okay... I guess. I just want all this ghost nonsense to be over with. Honestly, I'm worried that another appearance by Amelia could hurt Maddie even more."

"Understandable," Chris nodded sympathetically. "But we'll do everything we can to make sure Amelia keeps her distance."

"I appreciate that." I sighed, feeling a bit skeptical.

"Speaking of Amelia," Chris began, "Our research today confirmed that the farmhouse was once part of the Laine estate."

"Really?" I asked curiously, raising an eyebrow. "How does that relate to Amelia?

"We're not sure yet, but we have suspicions. Her mother

was named Allison... and Amelia was born in the house. Do you want to see her birth certificate?"

"Show me," I replied, curious about this new revelation.

Chris pulled a folder from his jacket and handed me the document. "Here... Amelia Luce, born on Valentine's Day in 1952, and the address for the birthplace is the same as the farmhouse."

I studied the document, amazed that there was tangible proof of Amelia's existence. "So, is this why she's haunting the place, because she was born here?"

"Not necessarily... check this out." Chris handed me a newspaper article about Amelia's and Allison's disappearance. "Amelia and her mom disappeared at the same time, and they never found any clues as to why," Chris continued, handing me another article from the folder.

I scanned the headlines and read the copy. "This is terrifying... could this happen to us?"

"Not likely. That was a different time with different circumstances," Chris said reassuringly, placing a hand around my waist. "We think there was a reason Allison and Amelia went missing. It's all speculation at this point but we're confident about our assumptions."

"Will your assumptions lead to something that will make Amelia to go away?" I asked, a bit cynically.

"It's part of a bigger puzzle we need to figure out. There's a reason she's trapped here, some conflict that she needs resolved before she can be at rest. I'm confident we'll figure that out."

I handed the documents to Chris, and he placed them in the folder, then stuffed it back into his jacket.

"Tomorrow, I have a meeting with the executive director of the local historical society, kind of a fact-finding mission with some accusations thrown in to see what reaction I get. The head guy has the same first and last name as the person who owns the farmhouse property. I suspect he's related."

"Mind if I tag along?" I asked, my curiosity piqued. "I'd like to hear the details myself, maybe confront him about Amelia haunting the place."

"I wouldn't have a problem with that," Chris agreed, surprised by my interest. "There's always strength in numbers, but promise me you'll follow my lead and not say anything that would piss him off. We need as much info as he can provide."

"I wouldn't do that - at least not unprovoked." I cocked my head playfully and smiled at the thought of a 'friendly' confrontation. "Can Maddie stay with Kat at your office?"

"Kat would love that, I'm sure. I'll let her know our plans."

As the sun dipped below the horizon and darkness began to envelop us, the fireflies grew bolder, their tiny lights dancing around us like celestial beings. The sound of rustling leaves and distant crickets created an almost serene atmosphere as we continued our walk.

"Evenings like this make me remember why I love fall," Chris mused, his breath visible in the crisp air.

"Me too," I agreed, feeling a sense of peace enveloping us as we strolled down the tree-covered road away from the farmhouse. In an instant, my thoughts turned to Amelia and her mom, Allison.

"I can't imagine what could have happened to make both

of them disappear," I said softly, my voice wavering a bit with emotion. "At least they were together when things happened. Allison didn't lose Amelia."

My eyes began to well up with tears at the thought of losing Maddie. Chris noticed the change in my demeanor and understood the direction of my thoughts.

"Sam, listen," Chris said earnestly, stopping in the middle of the road to face me. "I know this may sound hollow, but everything happens for a reason, and we never really face anything alone. Remember when I told you about that 'inner light' in all of us?"

I nodded 'yes' in response, unable to speak.

"That light never fades - not in Maddie, not in you, not in any of us. It's a feeling - a belief that there is something bigger than us that understands and has a purpose in everything that happens, both good and bad. You'll never be alone, Sam, and Maddie will always live within you."

"Thanks," I said softly, the usual reply to anyone offering support or sympathy for the inevitable. "I haven't talked about this with anyone, and I know I need to deal with it... like tell someone how I feel about losing Maddie. I just haven't trusted anyone enough to open up about it."

"I'm a good listener," he replied softly, reaching out to brush a stray lock of hair behind my ear. The gesture was surprisingly intimate, and I felt a warmth run through me.

The branches of the trees above us began to move; their leaves a kaleidoscope of reds, oranges, and yellows dancing in the wind. The sight of them stirred something within me, a deep longing for connection... for hope. Tears pricked at the corners of my eyes, and before I knew it, they were streaming down my cheeks. Chris immediately enveloped me in a comforting embrace, his strong arms providing a sense of safety I hadn't felt in a long time.

"Hey, it's going to be okay," he reassured me gently, lifting my chin so our eyes met. He smiled warmly, brushing a tear from my cheek. "Trust me."

As if on cue, the fireflies began to circle around us, their tiny lights illuminating the moment like a scene from a fairy tale. I could feel the electricity between us, the magnetic pull that had always been there. Our lips were inches apart when a sharp sound shattered the moment. We both flinched as Chris pulled out his phone, frowning at the screen.

"Damn it," he muttered before answering. "Norman? What's going on?"

"We have activity!" Norman's voice crackled through the speaker. I felt a chill run through me, and it wasn't from the cool evening air.

"Where's Maddie?" Chris demanded, concern etching lines in his face.

"She's here with us in the van."

"Stay put. We're heading that way."

My heart raced as we sprinted up the shadowy road. The darkness seemed to close in around us, heightening my fear with every step. Within minutes, I could see Norman, Kat, and Maddie huddled together in the back of the van, their faces illuminated by the eerie glow of the video monitors. I could tell Maddie was afraid, and as Chris and I climbed inside, my attention turned to her.

"Are you okay?" I asked, my breath ragged from our

sprint. She nodded, still gripping Kat's hand tightly.

"Look," Norman pointed to one of the screens. In the dim twilight, shadowy figures moved beyond the fence line behind the field. "Something or someone's out there."

"Let me see," Chris said, leaning over to get a better look at the monitor. I stared at the screen, trying to make sense of the shifting darkness.

"Let's check it out," Chris said with determination. "Sam, are you ok to come with me?"

"I... I guess so," I replied with a nod, and we stepped out the back of the van into the chilling twilight.

"Stay in here, all of you. Norman, hit record," Chris ordered.

"Recording -"

"Be careful," Kat interrupted, in a high-pitched squeal.

The van door closed behind us with a soft thud as we cautiously crept through the darkness. My heart pounded in my chest. Every creak, every rustle of leaves seemed amplified in the eerie silence. Chris picked up an old shovel leaning against the barn, gripping it tightly as if preparing for battle. It wasn't much of a weapon, but it was better than nothing.

"Those shadows...they're not just trees swaying in the wind, are they?" I asked, my voice trembling.

"Doesn't look like it... stay close." Chris's grip tightened on the shovel as he entered the grassy field.

"You don't have to ask me twice," I replied anxiously.

We moved cautiously; our footsteps muffled by the damp grass. The sound of distant rustling leaves mixed with our own labored breaths.

"Do you think this is a spirit thing like Amelia?" I asked, trying to keep my voice steady.

"Right now, I don't know what to think." I could hear the uncertainty in his voice which did little to calm my mounting anxiety. "I wish I'd brought a flashlight."

We moved closer to the tree line by the back fence. The shadows around us seemed to grow larger and more ominous. My breaths came in short gasps as fear threatened to consume me. Every rustle of leaves, every snap of a twig set my nerves on edge.

"Wait," Chris whispered suddenly, stopping in his tracks. "Do you hear that?"

I stopped, listening for anything different than the natural sounds of the night, and then I heard it: a low, guttural growl, echoing through the darkness.

"What the hell is that?" I gasped, terror seizing my throat.

"I don't know."

We stood there, frozen in fear, clutching each other as the growling grew louder, closer. The shadows danced and twisted around us, taking on sinister forms that filled my imagination with unspeakable horrors.

"Stay behind me, Sam," Chris ordered, wielding the shovel like a protective barrier between us and the unknown.

The growling intensified, mixed now with heavy, labored breathing. The very air vibrated with primal malice, and in that moment, I knew without a doubt that something monstrous lurked just out of sight.

"Did you see that?"

Chris's eyes scanned the shadows. I squinted, trying

to make out the shape that caught his attention. There, against the dark of the woods, I could see something moving... something big.

"I see it!" I whispered urgently, pointing at the shadowy figure darting through the trees just beyond the fence line. "Is that a wolf?"

"Maybe," Chris replied, gripping the shovel tightly. "But it's...it's bigger than a wolf... damn," he muttered under his breath.

We listened in horror as the creature snarled and growled, punctuated by an occasional gut-wrenching howl.

"Look at it," Chris whispered, his voice tight. "It's like something out of a nightmare."

The creature was massive, its body covered in coarse fur that seemed to shift and shimmer in the dim light. Its eyes were dark and hollow, like twin voids that threatened to swallow us whole. It snorted and growled; saliva dripping from its razor-sharp fangs.

My heart pounded in my chest as I glanced frantically around, the creature's sounds rendering the woods even more ominous than before. That's when I saw her – a small figure darting between trees, her white dress a stark contrast to the shadows that enveloped her.

"Oh my God, Chris, look!" I cried out, my voice barely more than a whisper. "It's Amelia... she's out there!"

Through the darkness, I could make out the fragile figure of Amelia, her ghostly form trembling with fear as she hid behind a tree. Her eyes, wide and panicked, met mine for a moment before she disappeared.

The monstrous creature turned its gaze toward us, its eyes gleaming with a primal hunger that sent ice-cold terror coursing through my veins. Slowly, deliberately, it began to move in our direction.

"Run, Sam!" Chris yelled, grabbing my hand, and pulling me along as we sprinted back toward the safety of the van.

My heart hammered against my chest as we raced through the field, the creature's growls and snarls growing louder with each passing second.

"It's too close!" I screamed, my breath ragged as we finally reached the van.

"Get in!"

Chris shoved me inside before climbing in. The door slammed shut just as the creature's snarls reached a fever pitch, drowning out all other sounds.

"Holy shit, you okay?" Norman asked, shocked by what he had witnessed.

"Y-yeah," I stammered, still trying to catch my breath.

Our hearts pounded in unison as we tried to process what had just transpired. Fear clung to us like a second skin.

"What the freak was that thing?" Kat's voice broke as she pleaded for an answer.

"It was huge!" Norman stammered, his hands shaking as he fumbled with a knob on the monitor. "It looked like a wolf, but...bigger."

"I've never seen anything like it," Chris admitted, his voice low and measured. "It was wolflike, but the size of it...it was more like a bear."

"Amelia..." Maddie whimpered, her eyes wide with fear.

"She's out there with that thing."

"Maddie, how do you know that?" I questioned, remembering the terrified look on Amelia's face as she hid in the woods.

A bloodcurdling scream pierced the air outside the van. It was Amelia, and the terror in her voice sent chills through me. My heart was in my throat as I looked at the others, fear etched on all our faces.

"Amelia!" I cried out, instinctively moving towards the door. Chris grabbed my arm, holding me back.

"Sam you can't!"

Maddie slumped to one side, her eyes rolling back as she fell into a trance. "Mama help me," she screamed, her voice deep desperate.

"Shit," Kat swore, rushing to Maddie's side. "Maddie, it's okay, you're okay."

Maddie was gone. Amelia's spirit controlled her body now, speaking through her, screaming, and begging for help. The hairs on the back of my neck stood up, and a cold sweat formed on my brow.

The air inside the van was damp and suffocating. I held Maddie's trembling body close, terrified by the sounds echoing from outside the van. Amelia's panicked cries pierced the air, mixed with the growls and snarls of the creature hunting her.

"Chris, we have to do something!" I shouted, my voice cracking. Norman's eyes were glued to the video screen, his fingers tapping furiously on the keyboard as he attempted to zoom in on the chase unfolding before our eyes.

"There's no time! It's almost on her," Chris replied, his eyes never leaving the screen. Maddie's body suddenly went rigid in my arms, her legs flailing as though she was running.

"Get away from me!" she shrieked, her eyes rolling back in her head until only the whites showed.

"Kat, help me hold her!" I cried out, as Maddie thrashed around wildly, desperately trying to break free from my grasp. Kat grabbed her legs, her own eyes wide with fear.

"Stay with us, Maddie!" she yelled, her voice shaking.

Maddie continued to fight an unseen battle, twisting, and flailing with clinched fists as her legs mimicked a desperate run. My gaze flicked to the video screen. Amelia's spirit, illuminated by the eerie glow of the infrared camera, was sprinting across the pasture towards the farmhouse. Behind her, the large, wolf-like creature closed in, its massive form a horrifying blur of darkness and malice.

"Oh my God, Amelia, please, run faster!" I pleaded, tears streaming down my cheeks as I watched the nightmarish scene unfold.

"Don't let this happen," Norman screamed as he gripped the edge of the screen.

"Dear God," Chris whispered, resigned to the outcome he believed was inevitable.

A sudden burst of light erupted from Amelia's spirit, filling the screen, and blinding us momentarily. When the light faded, Amelia's form had vanished, replaced by thousands of tiny, glowing particles that swirled in the air like fireflies.

"What just happened?" Kat asked, astonished.

"I'm not sure," Chris replied, his face pale as he stared at the screen. "I think we just lost Amelia." A tangible sadness overwhelmed us, threatening to rip our hearts from our chests. "Amelia," I whispered into the darkness, tears streaming down my face as hopelessness took hold.

"Wait, look outside!" Chris suddenly shouted, pointing towards the front windshield. A mesmerizing swarm of glowing particles surrounded the van, casting an eerie luminescence throughout the interior.

"Those are Amelia's remains," Kat said, her voice trembling. "But why are they surrounding us?"

"Maybe she's still with us," I suggested, hope flickering briefly within me.

"Maybe that thing wants more than just her," Chris countered darkly.

As if on cue, the creature let out a guttural growl and charged us, its massive form barreling through the darkness like a freight train. I tried to brace for the impact, though I knew it would be futile. We were trapped inside this tin can, faced with an evil beyond comprehension.

"Amelia, if you're still with us, we need your help!" Chris screamed, his voice reverberating against the van's walls. The fireflies seemed to pulse and shimmer in response, their light intensifying for a moment before fading to their usual glow.

"Look!" Kat shouted, pointing at the video screen. The creature had stopped in its tracks, its massive form mere inches from the van. It sniffed the air cautiously, as though it could sense the barrier that stood between us.

"Is it... leaving?" I asked, my heart daring to hope for a

moment of reprieve.

"No, it's just biding its time," Chris replied grimly.

The van shuddered violently, and my heart raced as the sound of scraping filled the air. The creature seemed to be everywhere at once, circling us like a predator playing with its prey. Norman screamed, his voice cracking with terror.

"Keep watching the screens," Chris ordered before leaping to the front seat. I held my breath, praying that he had a plan to save us.

"Oh my God, Chris!" Kat screamed in a shrill voice. The enormous head and dark eyes of the creature filled the windshield, looking like something straight from the depths of hell. Chris frantically searched for anything he might use as a weapon, but it was too late. With one enormous bound, the creature lunged, crashing through the windshield, showering us all with shards of broken glass. Maddie let out a blood-curdling scream that seemed to pierce the very fabric of reality. In that instant, everything fell silent. The creature and its nightmarish presence vanished as if they had never existed.

Chris crouched motionless in the front seat, waiting for the lethal assault that never came. He slowly lowered his arms and turned to face us, his face pale and white.

"Is...is it gone?" I whispered, trembling as I clutched Maddie tightly. She was crying, her small body wracked with sobs. Kat was crying too, and for once, she had nothing to say.

"I think it's gone," Chris stated, his voice barely a whisper as he leaned to look through the broken front windshield.

"Sam, are you and Maddie okay?" He turned and directed

his gaze towards us, concern etched on his face.

"I... I think so," I stammered, trying to comfort Maddie as best as I could.

"Norman, any sign of that thing on the screen?" Chris asked, desperate for answers.

"Nothing," Norman replied. "It's like it just... vanished."

With a deep breath, Chris crawled over us and opened the van's back door, peering out into the darkness. He stepped out, his body tense and alert to any sign of danger. I watched as Norman joined him, his lanky frame shaking slightly. Together, they circled the van, looking for any sign of the creature that had created such havoc. I hesitated for a moment before stepping out into the night. Kat and Maddie joined me, all three of us clinging to each other for support. My breath caught in my throat at the sight of the deep claw marks etched into the door and the long scratches that marred the van's sides. The front windshield was nothing but a jagged hole, glass littering the hood like fallen stars.

"Damn," Norman muttered, running his hand along a deep scar, clearly unnerved. "This is bad."

Chris stared towards the open field behind the barn. I couldn't help but follow his gaze, my eyes landing on a mesmerizing sight – a column of light swirled upward into the night sky. Fireflies danced within the luminescent pillar, their glow like tiny embers from a fire.

"Wow," Kat breathed, wiping her tears as she stood transfixed by the ethereal sight.

"Sam," Chris said, turning to me with sadness in his eyes. "I think we just learned how Amelia died."

I glanced at him, my eyes wide. "I know... that thing killed her!"

"I don't think so," Chris replied, shaking his head. "I think she jumped into the well to get away from it."

"Into the *well?*" I asked, my stomach twisting with dread as I imagined Amelia's final moments, terrified and alone, in the depths of a watery grave. "Amelia," I whispered into the void, hoping beyond hope that she could hear me. "I'm so sorry."

The silence that surrounded us was once again punctuated by the distant echo of a young girl's crying, a haunting reminder that the line between the living and the dead could be easily crossed.

Chapter Ten

The Cool Kat Club

I listened as Maddie's laughter filled the small office of the Leesburg Ghost Tours, her eyes twinkling with delight at the sight of Kat sitting on the desk wearing her motorcycle helmet. The black headgear was a perfect match to her black scooter, and ever true to her edgy personality, it featured large cat ears sticking out from the top.

"Really, Kat?" Chris asked, unable to suppress a smirk. "Why are you wearing that inside?"

Hey, after that thing attacked us last night, I'm not taking any chances," she replies defiantly. "Safety first, right?"

I chuckled, nodding my agreement. "Maybe it's not such a bad idea."

"Whatever you say," Chris conceded, shaking his head with a smile. "We should be back in an hour or so after our meeting with George. You two will be okay here?"

"Of course," Kat said, scooping up Maddie and settling her on her lap. "We're gonna have some fun, huh Maddie." Maddie nodded in agreement.

With that, Chris and I left the office and made our way

down the stairs, passing through the aromatic restaurant. My stomach growled, reminding me how hungry I was.

"Ugh, everything smells so good, doesn't it? I'm starving."

"We'll grab a bite after our meeting," he suggested, holding the door open for me as we stepped outside onto King Street. I glanced over at him, curious about our destination. "So, where are we heading?"

"George should be waiting for us at the Market House, just up the street," Chris explained as we walked in the direction of the courthouse. "The building was an old firehouse built around 1830 but it's a museum now. George said he had some business to tend to there and figured it was as good a place as any to meet."

"The Historical Society doesn't have an office?" I questioned.

"Not really. They have monthly public meetings at the library, and sometimes members meet at an old train depot they're restoring. Nothing official."

"I see. Is there anything I should know about George before we meet?" I ask, eager for any insight that might help me navigate the encounter.

Chris considered my question for a moment before answering. "Well, he's in a wheelchair, and he can be a bit...pompous," Chris explained. "The way he sits in his chair makes him seem like he's on a throne or something." I couldn't help but laugh at the mental image that description conjured up.

"Alright, King George it is," I said with a grin as we entered the dimly lit museum.

Immediately, I was struck by the history that surrounded

us. The walls were adorned with old photographs documenting the volunteer firefighters of Leesburg, and various pieces of antique fire equipment were scattered throughout the space. It felt like we stepped back in time.

The sound of an electric motor spinning reached my ears, and I turned to see George approaching from the back of the room on his motorized wheelchair. It's clear that Chris was right; with his regal bearing and commanding presence, George did indeed look like a king surveying his domain from atop his mobile throne. I stifled a giggle as he approached.

"Ah, Chris, good to see you again," George called out as he rolled up. It was clear from his tone that he was used to being in control of any situation.

"George... good to see you as well, and thanks for meeting with us," Chris replied, offering a friendly smile. I held my breath, unsure of what to expect from this enigmatic figure.

"Of course," George replied, his voice conveying a sense of authority. "I'm always willing to share my knowledge with a fellow history enthusiast." His eyes flicked briefly in my direction before returning to Chris. "I'm here to select some photographs for the Heritage Breakfast we're hosting in tomorrow... you know, our annual fundraiser for the Historical Society. Seems my help hasn't shown up yet." He sighed in annoyance.

"Sorry to hear that," Chris replied sympathetically. "We're happy to lend a hand if you need it."

"Thanks, but no thanks," George dismissed the offer with a wave of his hand. "It'll all get sorted out eventually." There was a brief pause before George chuckled and continued, "So, how goes the ghost hunting business? Still at it, are you?"

"Actually, that's why we're here," Chris explained, trying to keep the conversation light. "Things have been busier than usual lately, and we're hoping you might be able to help us out with some historical context."

George raised a skeptical eyebrow, clearly amused. "Oh? And what sort of assistance do you think I can provide?"

I couldn't help but feel a bit miffed at being ignored, but I reminded myself that we were there to gather information, not make friends.

"Ever the skeptic, huh?" Chris said with a smile. "Well, our recent investigations have led us to believe there might be a connection to some local history. We thought your expertise could come in handy."

"Alright, I'll bite," George acquiesced, his curiosity getting the better of him. "What exactly are you looking for from me?"

"Answers about a spirit," Chris stated simply, his expression serious.

"Ha!" George scoffed, clearly not buying it. "And you think I can provide these 'answers'? You really are grasping at straws, aren't you?"

"Maybe," Chris admitted, undeterred by George's skepticism.

"Very well," George said with a resigned sigh. "Let's hear what you've got."

Realizing he hadn't introduced me yet, Chris turned to me and began, "George, I'd like you to meet—"

"Samantha," George interrupted, a knowing glint in his eye. "You're the woman staying at my farmhouse with your daughter, aren't you? Maddie, is it?"

I blinked, taken aback by his knowledge of our living situation. "Yes, that's right. I didn't realize you were the owner."

"Technically speaking, yes," George replied, leaning back in his wheelchair. "The property was passed down from my father, but it's still controlled by the Laine Foundation. I must say, I'm rather surprised they demanded you be allowed to stay there. The place has been emptied for nearly sixty years."

"It's actually quite comfortable," I said, trying to hide my uneasiness with the conversation. "We're fortunate that my work made the arrangements for us to stay at the farmhouse."

"Indeed. You must know some important people to have been granted access like that," he mused, giving me a scrutinizing look. "The Foundation informed me you'd be occupying the residence for a short time but didn't provide much in the way of details."

"Actually," Chris interjected, "Sam and her daughter just needed a break from the city. Maddie's not feeling great, and they were looking for a quieter place."

"Ah, I see," George replied, his tone dismissive. "So, what 'answers' are you hoping I can provide?"

"We're curious about the history of the farmhouse," Chris began, shifting the conversation to our main reason for meeting with George. "I wanted to ask you about your father's connection to it, and specifically about his relationship with Lawrence Laine."

"Lawrence Laine," George muttered, running a hand through his thinning hair. "Quite the character, that one. Played an important role in Leesburg's history, as I'm sure you know."

"Of course," Chris agreed. "We're aware he was a successful TV and radio personality who had the large estate outside of town. What we don't know is how your father came to own a piece of that property, and the farmhouse."

"Ah, yes," George said, leaning back in his wheelchair. "My father and Lawrence were lifelong friends. They grew up together in West Virginia, long before Lawrence found fame. They served in the military together during the war, and Lawrence worked on an armed forces radio show that became quite popular. It was the springboard for his career."

"Really?" I asked, intrigued by this new information.

"Indeed," George continued, sounding irritated at my interruption of his thought process. "After the war, my father worked for Lawrence for the rest of his life, remaining a loyal friend until Lawrence passed away in the 1980's."

Chris pressed on, attempting to keep the conversation focused. "Why did your father become the owner of the farmhouse and that small piece of land?"

George's eyes narrowed, as if he were considering whether to share this information. Finally, he sighed. "I honestly don't know for certain. I can only assume it was a gift from Lawrence to my father as a token of gratitude for his loyalty over the years."

"Did your father ever live in the farmhouse?" I asked, trying to get a better understanding of the situation.

"No," George answered curtly. "He wanted nothing to do with it. That's why the place has been empty and in disrepair for so many years."

"Seems like an odd gift to give someone who didn't want it," Chris mused, his tone a little suspicious.

George bristled at the comment. "And why is it that you're so interested, Mr. Paranormal Investigator?"

"Sam here contacted me about some strange occurrences at the house," Chris explained, ignoring George's sarcastic jab. "She's been experiencing things that can't be easily explained."

"Ah, yes," George said with a smirk, "the old 'haunted house' routine. I've heard it all before, you know. People come to this town looking for a good scare, and they're rarely disappointed."

"Except this isn't just a scare, George," Chris countered. "We've encountered something that we can't explain – an apparition of a little girl named Amelia."

For a moment, the condescending grin left George's face, replaced by genuine surprise. But then he chuckled and shook his head. "Chris, my boy, you never cease to amaze me with your wild imagination. Come on, you don't really believe that nonsense, do you?"

"Actually, yes," I interjected, my voice firm. "A little girl named Amelia has appeared several times and has been affecting Maddie."

George burst into laughter, dismissing our claims as

ludicrous.

"George, I'm telling you —" I tried to protest, but Chris quickly intervened, giving me a reassuring glance.

"Whether you believe us or not, the fact remains that something is happening at that house," Chris declared, his voice filled with determination. "And if you know anything about its history, you owe it to us to share that information."

"I owe it to you, huh," George conceded, still smirking. "Fine, but if you think I have any information on a supposed ghost, you're sorely mistaken."

"Have you ever heard the name Allison Luce?" Chris asked, his tone softening slightly. "Our research shows she once lived in the farmhouse with her daughter Amelia."

"Ah, yes, those names do sound familiar," George admitted, though he seemed uneasy discussing them. "My father mentioned them a few times over the years, but I never knew any details about them."

"Does anything come to mind about their disappearance in the '60s?" Chris pressed.

"Interesting that you know about that...you've done your homework," George smirked, as he shifted in his wheelchair and flicked a switch to power it towards another part of the room. Chris and I exchanged glances before following him, both curious and frustrated by his evasiveness.

"I was only six when they disappeared" George said, his gaze moving around the room, avoiding eye contact. "I never knew why they were connected to the farmhouse, but I do remember all the police activity back then."

"Did your father ever talk about it?" Chris asked, trying

to get more information.

Spinning his chair around to face us, George's face hardened. "No," he said abruptly, offering nothing else on the matter.

I could feel my frustration mounting, but I tried to keep my emotions in check. "George, we're trying to understand what's happening in that house," I said, desperation creeping into my voice. "We need to know if the spirit we've encountered is the same Amelia that disappeared."

"Come now, Samantha," George chuckled sarcastically as he rolled his wheelchair a few inches closer to us. "Do you honestly expect me to believe that Amelia's ghost is haunting the farmhouse? The missing girl from decades ago?"

"Actually, yes," Chris replied firmly, locking eyes with George. "I think it's more than possible, considering everything we've learned."

"Look, I've told you everything I know," George insisted, irritation seeping through his words. "If my father knew anything, he took it to his grave. You're on your own with this one."

Surrounded by the dusty artifacts and fading photographs of Leesburg's past, we found ourselves in a stalemate. George Benningly Jr., a mystery himself, was both a valuable informant and an impediment in our search for answers.

"Alright, George," Chris sighed, realizing we weren't going to get any further on the topic. "We'll just have to look elsewhere for information."

"Good luck with that," George responded, his voice

dripping with sarcasm. "I'm sure you'll find a way to spin this into another one of your ghost stories for the tour."

"Really, George?" Chris couldn't help but scoff at the older man's condescending tone. "You think we're making all of this up?"

"Your line of work does tend to rely on such things," George retorted as he leaned back in his chair, a smug smile curling the corners of his lips. "I suppose that from your perspective as a paranormal investigator, anything is fair game. But from a historical point of view, it's just nonsense." George turned his attention to me, his dark gaze scrutinizing my face. "Samantha, I'm sure you've found things to entertain yourself with during your short stay in town. Many women around here seem to find Chris quite...attractive, and I think you share in that assessment...am I right, my dear?"

My face flushed with anger at his insinuation, and I clenched my fists at my sides. "You're unbelievable," I snapped, unable to hold my tongue any longer. "Do you really think I would make up a story about my daughter being tormented by a ghost just to get some attention? We were attacked by something last night – something unnatural!"

Chris placed a steadying hand on my arm, cutting off my tirade. He calmly explained the encounter with the wolf-like creature that attacked us the night before. "Amelia was present when it happened, and I think it was a spiritual event."

"Of course, you think that," George said dismissively, waving a hand as if swatting away an annoying fly. "I'm sure that must have been terrifying. But do you really expect me to believe it was a ghost?"

"Chris thinks it could be connected to the spiritual world," I interjected, glaring daggers at the smug historian. "And considering what we've experienced so far, I'm inclined to trust his judgment."

"Of course, you do," George replied, rolling his eyes. "Well, if you were indeed attacked by an animal, let me offer you an alternative explanation. When Lawrence Laine lived at the estate, he was known for his love of African safaris and exotic animals. In fact, he kept several wild creatures on the property as part of his passion for hunting. If you were indeed attacked by some animal, it's likely the descendant of one of those beasts. They may have escaped during one of Laine's hunts and bred in the surrounding woods over the years. So, my advice to you is to avoid taking any more late-night strolls."

His words carried a dark undertone, and I couldn't help but shudder at the thought of wild, dangerous animals lurking in the shadows around the farmhouse. But was it really a more plausible explanation than what we'd seen and felt for ourselves?

"Fine," I conceded, my voice tight with frustration. "No more walks in the woods. But don't think for one moment that we're going to let this go."

"Suit yourself," George said, his lips twisting into a cruel smile. "Just remember, some things are better left undisturbed."

Chris and I exchanged awkward looks, both of us at a loss for words.

"Your little chat with me this morning has been most entertaining, but I really have nothing more to offer you historically," George said, his tone dripping with condescension. "It's been a pleasant break from my usual routine."

"Thank you for your time, George," Chris replied, his voice strained but polite. "I'm glad we could provide some levity to your day."

George maneuvered his wheelchair towards the exit, pausing as he reached the door. He turned to face us, his expression a mix of annoyance and something else I couldn't quite place. "Samantha, do enjoy your time at the farmhouse, and I truly hope Maddie feels better soon," he said, almost sounding genuine.

Then, he looked at Chris, his eyes narrowing. "A word of advice, Chris. Don't dig too deeply into the history of the farmhouse or those involved. The Laine Foundation has graciously allowed Samantha and Maddie to be their guests, and I would hate for anything to jeopardize that hospitality."

"Of course," Chris agreed, though I knew he had no intention of dropping the matter.

"Enjoy your ghostly adventures at the farmhouse, Chris," George continued, rolling his eyes. "I'm sure they will provide you with plenty of fodder for another one of your money-making ghost tour ventures."

Without waiting for a response, George turned his attention to me, giving me a knowing wink. "And Samantha, enjoy your time with Chris. You wouldn't be the first woman in town to find him... interesting."

With that parting shot, George cackled loudly and exited through the front door, leaving us standing in the now-empty museum. My face burned with anger, and I felt the familiar sting of tears threatening to spill over.

"What an ass!" I exploded, my fists clenched. Chris stepped closer, placing a comforting arm around me.

"Told you he was full of himself," he said gently. "He was just trying to rattle us because he knows we're on to something... it's his way of throwing us off."

"Ugh," I groaned, forcing myself to take a deep breath and regain my composure. "It's just so infuriating."

Still fuming from our encounter with George, Chris and I made our way up King Street to join Kat and Maddie. The tension I felt was replaced by a mixture of amusement and surprise as we walked through the office door. In the middle of the floor sat Maddie, across from Kat, wearing a tin foil hat complete with molded cat ears, just like Kat's helmet. To top it off, my sweet little girl was donning makeup on her eyes and lips that mirrored Kat's style.

"Really, Kat?" Chris asked, raising an eyebrow. Kat shrugged sheepishly, her grin wide and infectious.

"Sorry," she said, not sounding sorry at all. "Maddie insisted on being part of the cool-Kat club."

I glanced at Chris, who seemed to be fighting back laughter, then turned my attention to Maddie. She looked so proud of herself, her face beaming with excitement. How could I be upset?

"Alright," I conceded, unable to keep the smile from my own face. "You two can be in the cool-Kat club together."

"Woohoo!" Maddie and Kat chorused, high fiving each

other.

"Where do we go from here?" I asked turning to Chris, feeling the frustration of our conversation with George resurfacing.

"Well, first things first," Chris replied, his eyes twinkling with mischief. "Lunch."

Chapter Eleven

A Birthday Party

February 15th, 1952

The grandeur of the Laine estate was on full display that afternoon, as the sprawling grounds were transformed into a lavish playground. A menagerie of colorful balloons swayed gently in the breeze, while tables laden with decadent treats and gleaming silverware glittered beneath the bright Virginia sun.

It was February 15th, 1952, and Laine had spared no expense in celebrating his daughter's ninth birthday. The sprawling estate buzzed with activity as guests mingled amidst the opulence, sipping cocktails, and nibbling on delicate hors d'oeuvres. Close friends and family mingled with show sponsors and members of the press, brought together to witness the extravagant spectacle of the young girl's special day.

"This party is a real blast, don't you think?" one guest remarked as she adjusted the pearls around her neck, the hem of her silk dress rustling softly in the breeze.

"Laine's outdone himself," replied another, taking a drag from his freshly lit cigarette. "Always one to put on a show."

Amidst the laughter and casual conversation, Laine stood tall, a dashing figure in his tailored suit and silk tie, expertly navigating the crowd of well-wishers and photographers. With a practiced smile, he led his beaming daughter around the estate's immaculately manicured lawns atop her new pony – a gift from her doting father. The click and flash of Variety magazine's photographers captured every moment, and Laine reveled in the attention, knowing full well that this would further cement his image as the perfect family man.

Lawrence stood tall among his friends and acquaintances; a cigar clenched between his teeth as he regaled them with stories of his latest television escapades. His eyes, however, remained keenly observant, flitting over the crowd like a hawk surveying its prey. The alcohol flowed freely, loosening tongues and inhibitions, but Lawrence maintained a careful balance between conviviality and control.

"Can you believe this?" Alba Weston muttered sarcastically under her breath, taking in the scene from behind a row of neatly trimmed hedges. She clutched her delicate shawl tighter around her shoulders, feeling out of place amid the extravagance. Laine continued to preen and pose for the cameras as her thoughts wandered to the run-down farmhouse, she had just left moments before.

"Quite the spectacle, isn't it?" A familiar voice interrupted her reverie, causing her to startle. George Benningly had sidled up beside her, nursing a tumbler of amber liquid.

"Hard to believe that just yesterday, another little

girl was born on this very property," Alba whispered conspiratorially, her eyes never leaving Laine as he basked in the attention.

"Adjacent property, technically." George replied tersely, his gaze fixed on his friend. "Best to keep that between us, don't you think?"

"I suppose," Alba agreed, but her heart ached for Allison and Amelia, hidden away in their quiet corner of the sprawling estate, unknown and unacknowledged by the man who should have been celebrating their existence.

Clouds of smoke filled the air, swirling and dissipating as Chesterfield cigarettes burned brightly between the fingers of nearly every guest. The scent of tobacco mingled with the aroma of fine spirits, laughter bubbling up from those who had indulged in one too many glasses of their favorite beverage. Despite the event being a child's birthday celebration, the atmosphere carried an undeniable air of adult sophistication.

Lawrence stood at the epicenter, flashing a pearly white smile towards everyone in attendance. Though it was his daughter's day to shine, he couldn't help but bask in the attention that came so easily to him. He was a master of public relations, always aware of how to play to his audience.

"Alba, I can't believe you're here!" Laine's wife Julia exclaimed as she approached, her voice filled with genuine surprise and warmth. Alba turned to her just in time to be swallowed by open arms. "Such a thoughtful gesture," she beamed, "having the person who brought our little angel into the world here on her special day."

Laine couldn't help but notice his wife's loud greeting of Weston, the midwife who had been present at the births of two of his children. He felt a twinge of suspicion, wondering why Alba had suddenly appeared at the party. His gaze followed George as he nodded to Julia and stepped away, pointing at his drink which needed attention. With practiced ease, Laine excused himself from the photographers and approached the pair, eager to eavesdrop on their exchange.

"Honey, you didn't tell me you invited Alba!" she said eagerly, looking at Lawrence as he approached.

"Actually, I'm as surprised as you are. I think it was probably George who arranged it," Laine interjected, feigning nonchalance. "I'm sure he wanted to include Alba in our birthday party for sentimental reasons."

"Well, I'm glad you came, Alba, and I appreciate you being here to help us celebrate," Julia continued. "Please enjoy yourself... we'll catch up on things later. I'm dying to know what you've been up to these past years." Julia hugged Alba one last time before turning her attention to other guests.

"Of course!" Alba agreed, watching the sea of floral dresses and flowing skirts part as Julia moved away.

"Mrs. Weston," Laine greeted Alba with a practiced smile, though his eyes betrayed a hint of unease. "I must say, I didn't expect to see you here today."

Alba swiveled around to face him. "Mr. Laine," she spoke steadily, "I've been staying with Allison for over a week now, at the farmhouse."

"Allison?" He asked in disbelief and his face betrayed his

surprise. "Why would you be staying with her?" Genuine worry overtook him as he waited for an answer.

"I thought George kept you in the loop about everything," Alba responded, surprised at Lawrence's ignorance of the situation.

Laine grimaced but his expression still held a hint of amusement. "I haven't spoken to George recently," he remarked dryly, "care to enlighten me?"

Alba's expression was unflinching despite the weight of what she carried within her. "There's something you should know." She paused, allowing the gravity of her words to sink in.

Lawrence motioned for her to follow and led her to a secluded corner of the garden, his eyes darting nervously around as they walked. "Okay, Alba," he began tersely, "what do I need to know?"

"Congratulations," she replied, her voice firm yet compassionate, "you have a new daughter. Her name is Amelia, born just yesterday."

"Amelia?" Laine scoffed, feigning ignorance as he glanced around at the gathered guests.

Laine's face contorted in disbelief, quickly followed by anger. "I don't know what you're talking about," he spat, denying any knowledge of the child. But Alba persisted.

"Please," Alba implored, her gaze unwavering. "There's no need for pretense with me. George made the arrangements for me to oversee Amelia's birth. Your denial won't change the truth," she said solemnly. "Amelia is your daughter, whether you acknowledge her or not."

For a moment, Laine's facade cracked, betraying the

guilt and fear that lay beneath. He knew the consequences of his actions; an illegitimate child would destroy everything he had built. In a fit of rage, he dismissed both Allison and Amelia, making it clear to Alba that they meant nothing to him.

"Even if I were the father," he sneered, "the world will never know. And neither will you." His eyes bore down menacingly upon her, leaving no doubt as to the gravity of his threat. Alba's heart sank as the reality of Lawrence's indifference became painfully clear.

"Lawrence," Alba continued, unwilling to let the matter rest, "I've seen firsthand how generous you are with your children." She gestured towards the birthday girl, who sat atop her brand-new pony, grinning ear-to-ear. "I can't help but wonder if this generosity will extend to all of your children."

"Ha!" Laine laughed, the sound hollow and devoid of any warmth. "I'm sure my daughter will tire of this new toy soon enough, just like all the rest." His dismissive tone made it clear that he saw Amelia as nothing more than an inconvenient truth, a blemish on his otherwise perfect life. He turned back to Alba, his smile fading into a cold, calculated sneer. "Allison and the child will be provided for, in exchange for their silence. And remember, Miss Weston, you owe me your loyalty as well." Laine held Alba's gaze without wavering, his eyes daring her to flinch. "Mark my words, Miss Weston, every gift and memory will wither away with the passing of time. You'd be wise to remember that."

"Lawrence!" a rotund man in a houndstooth jacket called

out from the sponsor group and began striding towards Laine with purpose. "I wanted to give your little girl something special for her birthday."

"Ah, Charles! Thank you," Laine said, accepting the small, wrapped gift with a gracious smile. He motioned towards the bar with a flourish. "Why don't you go grab yourself a drink?" As Charles wove his way through the crowd, Laine turned to Alba, who had been watching their exchange with interest.

"Here," he said, thrusting the gift into Alba's hands. "Give this to Allison for the child. Since you seem so concerned about my generosity, I think I'll let you play the part of benefactor."

"If you insist," Alba replied, her voice tight but controlled. She knew she needed to tread lightly around Laine.

"Tell Allison that my congratulations and best wishes are also included," Laine continued, irritation lacing his words.

"Actually, Lawrence," Alba ventured hesitantly, "Allison mentioned how much she misses you. She hopes you might find the time to visit her and see your new daughter."

"Is that so?" Laine sneered, his eyes narrowing. "Well, Miss Weston, I don't think that would be wise, so you can let Allison know she shouldn't hold her breath." With that, he turned on his heel and stalked away.

Alba studied the package in her grasp. The box was decorated with pink paper and tied with a delicate, red bow. On the back was an adhesive label that indicated who had given the present, as well as the logo of Laine's new sponsor.

"Ligget and Myers Tobacco Company - Such

a thoughtful gesture." Alba murmured to herself sarcastically.

Curious, Alba peeled away the wrapping paper. Inside, nestled in a velvet box, was a beautifully adorned golden locket. It was an ideal gift for a child, something that could hold significance if given with enough love and care. The cruel irony of it all didn't escape her: Laine had handed over the present without any notion of what was inside. A beautiful golden locket, intended as a token of love from a father who would never acknowledge his own child.

"Not much sentiment there," she mused as she looked at the delicate piece of jewelry. Still, with a mother's love, it might find its place in a young girl's heart one day. She folded up the paper and tucked the box into her purse, vowing to lie to Allison and tell her that the necklace was given with love. The fate of Allison and Amelia hung precariously in the balance, their futures intertwined with the whims of a man who cared only for himself.

»—•—«

Laine's face flushed with anger as he cornered George Benningly next to the massive stone fireplace in the grand living room. The flickering light from the fire cast ominous shadows across their faces as they argued in hushed tones.

"George, what in the hell were you thinking, bringing Weston here?" Laine hissed, clutching his glass of bourbon so tightly it threatened to shatter.

"She insisted on coming," George replied, his voice

steady despite Laine's fury. "She thought, being a licensed midwife and all, it was her job to let you know about the birth. Plus, she'd been there for your other kids, so it seemed appropriate."

"Appropriate?" Laine scoffed, downing the rest of his drink in one gulp. "You know damn well the press is swarming this place, and now I have to deal with questions about her being here?"

"Don't worry, Lawrence, nobody's onto anything," George comforted him. "Albas got the knack for keeping things hush-hush."

"Hush-hush?" Laine repeated, his voice rising in agitation. "She practically threw the news in my face without any concern for who might overhear! You need to get her away from this party, before my wife gets suspicious and starts asking questions."

"Alright, Lawrence, just calm down. I'll handle it," George said, placating his irate friend.

A photographer from Variety magazine approached, asking for another photo of Laine with his birthday girl atop her new pony - this time with other dignitaries attending the party. Laine smirked at George as he patted him on the shoulder. "Ever the family man... loved by all," he muttered sarcastically before plastering on a smile and walking away with the eager photographer.

George downed his mixed drink, a blend of tequila and lime juice that had a tart kick to it, and scanned the crowd for Alba. The light from the chandeliers cast an elegant pattern over everything and everyone, like some mystical spell. He found her standing near the buffet table, gazing down at the enormous spread of exquisite cuisine. He could see the conflict in her eyes and approached her cautiously. Every detail of her face was visible in his mind's eye: the furrow of her brow, the tiny creases around her eyes, and even the way her lips seemed to purse together in contemplation.

"Alba, we need to talk," George said quietly as he joined her at the table. Alba looked up, her eyes brimming with tears.

"George, you won't believe what Lawrence told me." She hissed, her voice quivering with anger. "He wants nothing to do with Allison or Amelia. They're nothing more than a nuisance to him and he could care less!"

"I'm not surprised," George admitted, his own voice heavy with regret. "You know how many other women have come and gone in his life since Allison took residence in the farmhouse. Allison means nothing to him, and the child is just a liability. I'm sure he'd like it all to just disappear."

"Disappear?" Alba repeated in disbelief and shock. "He's not even willing to acknowledge Amelia, not even to Allison?"

"Alba, you can't push this any further," George warned, his demeanor darkening. "You've done your job as asked. Now it's time for you to keep quiet about it and leave."

"Leave?" Alba asked, her eyes widening. "I thought I was going to be here for a while to help out... the girl was just born yesterday!"

"Lawrence wants you gone," George explained, his voice cold. "I'll request a driver to take you to the airport. You can catch a flight back to New York tonight."

"George, I can't just abandon them!" Alba protested, desperation etched across her face.

"I'm sorry," George said, softening slightly. "I can't go against Lawrence, and he feels threatened. I have to do as he asks."

With that, George escorted a distraught Alba to the front of the estate and motioned for a gray limousine parked at the end of the driveway. After a brief exchange of words with the driver, he turned and nodded in Alba's direction. "Have a safe trip back... I'll be in touch," he offered, before turning to walk inside and rejoin the party.

Alba's heart weighed heavy as she sat in the backseat of the sleek gray car. She felt disappointed and sad, as if a dark cloud had descended upon her soul. She glanced around at the opulent estate, taking in its immaculate gardens, pristine white fences, and vibrant blooms one last time. It was a stark contrast to the despair that now consumed her.

Her thoughts drifted back to her arrival at the event, a hopeful woman, eager to share the news of Amelia's birth with Lawrence Laine. That hope had been cruelly snuffed out by the indifference and disdain he had displayed. Alba's hands clenched into fists as she fought back tears, her worry for Allison and Amelia growing by the second.

"Miss Weston, I'll have you at the airport shortly," the driver informed her, his voice devoid of emotion.

"Thank you," she murmured as she glanced out the window.

The car picked up speed, leaving behind the sprawling property and the lavish birthday party still in full swing.

The laughter and merriment of the guests were now just a distant echo, replaced by a haunting silence that filled the vehicle. Alba watched as the lush green landscape rolled past. Her thoughts were consumed with worry for Allison and Amelia, left to navigate the treacherous waters of life under Lawrence Laine's control.

"God, please take care of them," She prayed quietly, hoping they would find a way to forge their own path, far from the indifference and cruelty that had been thrust upon them.

Chapter Twelve

The Letter

The sun hung low in the sky, casting long shadows across the lush, green grass surrounding the old farmhouse. Leaves rustled in the gentle breeze, and the air was crisp with the scent of autumn. Chris stood next to Norman, who was eager to show off his latest creation: an electric fence designed to keep wild creatures at bay.

"Check this out," Norman said, his glasses glinting in the sunlight as he tossed a tree branch against the wires. The branch sizzled and smoked as electricity coursed through it, and it fell to the ground charred and smoldering. Norman's chest puffed up with pride, his nerdy demeanor more apparent than ever.

"Isn't that a bit... much?" Chris asked skeptically, following the fence line with his gaze as it snaked around the van and across the front of the farmhouse towards the barn. "How are we supposed to get in and out of the house with this thing in the way?"

Norman's face flushed as he realized his oversight. "Um, yeah, I'll need to tweak that," he said, scratching his head. "But no worries, I'll have it sorted out by tonight."

"Is there a way to turn it on and off?" Chris inquired further.

"Uh... not yet," Norman admitted sheepishly. "But like I said, I'll fix it."

Chris couldn't help but smile at Norman's enthusiasm. It was well intended, if not practical.

"Hey, Chris, did you see any animal tracks around the van? I mean, after that whole wolf thing last night, I thought there'd be tracks all over the place, but I haven't seen any."

"Come to think of it, neither have I," Chris replied, raising an eyebrow. "You know, I've got a feeling our run-in with that creature was more on the supernatural side... not just your typical beast wandering in from the woods. That would explain why it just vanished the way it did."

Norman nodded in agreement. "Yeah, makes sense. It sure packed a punch though for a spook." He looked towards the hasty repairs made to the shattered windshield, now covered in cardboard and duct tape. Changing the subject, he continued. "How did the meeting with George go?"

"Pretty much how I figured it would go," Chris said with a sigh. "George was dismissive and talked down to us. He didn't give us any real info on why Allison and Amelia were here."

"No surprise there," Norman grumbled. "I'm still thinking spiritual encounters will tell us more than any historian ever could."

Chris gave a slow nod, mulling over Norman's point. "Yeah, you're onto something with that line of thinking. Let's just keep our heads in the game and be ready for whatever gets thrown our way next."

⋙ ⋘

I waved Chris over to where Kat, Maddie and I were sitting in the grassy field next to the barn. Kat was still rocking that cat-eared helmet, and Maddie had her tin foil hat on like a boss.

"Hey, Chris, come join us!" I called out, holding a soft, worn quilt in my hands.

The air was crisp and carried the scent of earth and decaying leaves, a bittersweet reminder of the changing seasons. I spread the old quilt on the ground, its faded colors and intricate patterns telling stories of a time long gone. Chris settled next to me, his expression a mix of curiosity and concern.

"Sam," he began hesitantly, "I hope you've recovered from last night's attack... It was scary, wasn't it?"

My heart sank just thinking about it, and I peeked at Maddie, who was happily occupied in the leaves. "Scary doesn't even cover it. We were lucky no one got hurt."

Chris looked out across the field, deep in thought, and didn't respond.

"I wouldn't mind a glass of wine right about now," I said, half-joking but also craving the comfort it would bring.

"Sounds like a good idea," Chris agreed, already pushing himself to his feet. "I'll grab some from the kitchen."

"Hold on a sec," Kat chimed in, throwing aside the leaves Maddie had used to bury her. "I'll grab it. I could go for a nip myself." With a determined stride, she headed off toward the kitchen, leaving Maddie alone in the pile.

Chris sat back down and turned his attention to me. "Sam, I understand your worry, but honestly, I don't think anybody's going to get hurt. Those spiritual run-ins we've had, they're kinda like replays... leftover vibes or energy showing us about Amelia and what went down."

"Replays?" I scoffed, my skepticism evident in both voice and posture. "Pretty realistic replays if you ask me. It felt more like were being hunted than shown someone's past. I'm about ready to grab Maddie and walk away from all this."

Chris gave in with a shrug. "You could. But I think you and Maddie are here for a reason, like you were destined to be here. Waking away now would leave Amelia's story untold, her spirit in limbo. We've already picked up some pretty good clues from these run-ins, and I think the roughest part is over... she revealed how she died. We just need to keep listening and observing. It'll all make sense sooner or later."

His words resonated with me, and despite my fears, I couldn't help but feel he was right.

"I guess so," I replied, my voice trembling just a bit. "Amelia deserves peace, just like Maddie deserves peace, especially now."

For a moment, I was content with the idea that a peaceful outcome for Maddie would be worth the risk. That bubble burst in an instant, as a scream that could wake the dead pierced the air. My heart practically jumped into my throat, thinking it was Amelia making her presence known.

FIREFLIES

Chris and I gave each other a wide-eyed, freaked-out look before realizing it wasn't Amelia making the racket – it was Maddie.

"Where is she?" I cried, panic rising in my chest. "She was just here!"

"It's coming from the barn!" Chris shouted, already sprinting towards the source. I followed close behind, my heart pounding.

We burst into the dimly lit room, and a chill ran through me. There, pinned against the back wall, was Maddie. Her eyes were wide with terror, and she clutched Amelia's book to her chest. At her feet, a massive black snake coiled ominously, its scales gleaming malevolently, its thick body tense and poised to strike. It was as though darkness itself had taken on a serpentine form and slithered into our lives.

"Mama!"

"Stay still, Maddie," I told her, trying to keep my voice calm. "We're here. We'll take care of it."

Chris lunged for a nearby wooden board, waving it at the snake to distract it and force it away. The snake hissed menacingly, its forked tongue darting out as it struck at the board. Instead of retreating, however, it moved closer to Maddie, encircling one of her small legs as if claiming her as its own.

"Norman!" Chris called out desperately, hoping he could help us. He appeared in the doorway, his eyes widening in horror at the scene before him.

"Snake!?" he squealed, his voice cracking. "No way, man! I can't... I just can't." He quickly hightailed it back out the door.

"Thanks for nothing," I muttered under my breath as I tried to think of a way to retrieve Maddie from the snake's grasp.

"Be brave, Maddie," I told her, tears welling in my eyes. "I love you so much."

"I love you too," she whimpered, her small body shaking with fear.

Suddenly, as if sensing the intimacy of our words, the snake released Maddie's leg and slithered away. It made its way up a ladder into the loft area of the barn and disappeared. Seizing the opportunity, I rushed forward and scooped Maddie into my arms. We raced out of the barn with Maddie still clutching the book tightly in her hands. Chris was hot on our heels.

"Are you okay?"

Maddie seemed weak, and her raspy breathing returned as she nodded, yes.

"Let's get you inside," I said, carrying her through the back kitchen door. Chris followed us inside, and watched as I laid Maddie on the bed in my room.

"Sweetie, can I have the book?" I gently tried to pull it from her tight grip.

"No," she whispered, and pulled it close to her chest, folding her arms around it like she would a doll.

"Why did you go into the barn?"

"I... I wanted Kat to read to me in the yard. Amelia told me to go get her book."

"Amelia," I thought, feeling my anger begin to boil. I clenched my jaw and fought back the words I wanted to scream at the top of my lungs. This spirit had once again put Maddie in harm's way.

"You should *never* go anywhere on this property by yourself, *do you understand me?* I exhaled heavily hoping to temper the volume of my voice. "Promise me you won't do that again." I spoke firmly, hoping she would understand the fear I felt.

"I promise," Maddie replied softly. "But you don't have to worry. I have Amelia. I'm never really alone."

I stared at her in disbelief. She honestly felt Amelia would always be with her, and I had no argument to counter that belief. My face flushed and I swallowed hard. Maddie was safe for now, and I needed to accept that.

"Do you want me to read to you from Amelia's book?"

"Please," she whispered, sounding tired and sleepy.

Maddie released her grasp, and I took the worn novel from her arms. I opened the book to a page bookmarked by several folded pieces of paper and began to read.

> *In the quiet hamlet of Whistler's Hollow, nestled beneath the watchful canopy of ancient oaks, there lived a woman shrouded in whispered tales and mystery, a solitary figure that the villagers regarded with a mixture of awe and dread. They knew her simply as 'the Witch', a name born of ignorance and fear, for her true essence was far removed from the malicious sorcery that their superstitions conjured.*
> *Beneath her ashen guise, she hid her own*

> *tragic story—a tale of a mother who had once lost her child to the cruel embrace of an unforgiving illness. Her grief had become the driving force behind her solitary life, her unyielding quest to safeguard the village's children from the same cruel fate.*

I let the book fall gently into my lap, and turned to look at Chris, wondering if he had been listening. His gaze met mine, and he nodded knowingly as I picked up the book and continued.

> *Within the heart of the dense forest, the Witch prepared for her nightly ritual. With a silver cauldron bubbling and a myriad of herbs and incantations at her fingertips, she cast her spells not to inflict harm, but to protect. Her heart ached for the children who feared her, their frightened glances like invisible chains binding her soul.*
> *Venturing out from the darkness of the woods, the transformed Witch encountered an assembly of children. Their wide eyes and hushed voices spoke volumes of their astonishment. "Fear not, dear children," she began, her voice a soothing river of reassurance. "I am not the villainous sorceress you've been told of. It is not you who should be wary, but the evil that hides in these woods."*

*She offered them vials filled with her protective
elixirs, inviting them to drink. "With these
potions," she explained, "you shall be shielded
from the malevolence that prowls in the night.
Carry them always, for I wish to protect you,
as once I wished to protect my own."*

Maddie's eyelids grew heavy and eventually closed, her breathing evening out as she drifted off to sleep. I put the book down and grabbed the folded papers to mark my progress. Curious, I opened them. Alba Weston had written a letter to Allison.

"Chris," I called out softly, trying not to wake Maddie. "Do you remember the name Alba Weston?"

"Um, yeah, I do," he replied. "She's the midwife listed on Amelia's birth certificate."

"Then you won't believe what I've found," I said, my voice shaking with excitement. "This is a letter from Alba to Allison, dated February 1952, shortly after Amelia's birth."

"Really?" Chris's eyes widened, and he leaned in closer. Together, we read through the letter, our excitement growing with each word.

My Dearest Allison,

*I hope this letter finds you in good health and
high spirits, though my own heart is heavy
as I pen these words. I write with the deepest*

remorse for my swift departure from you and Amelia, and with an ache that only the written word can mend. You must know that my exit was not of my own accord; it was Lawrence who, with his harsh words, insisted I leave so abruptly. It was not a choice I made willingly.

I yearned for more time with you, Allison, and with your sweet infant Amelia. Bringing her into this world, as I had the privilege of doing, was a moment of joy that has touched my soul profoundly. She is a beautiful child, a testament to your enduring love, and I know she is destined for greatness. But unfortunately, Lawrence's shadow looms, and I must share with you the reason for my hastened departure.

In the brightly lit corners of that ill-fated afternoon, I found myself face to face with Lawrence, his voice dripping with venom and his threats echoing through my very being. He warned me never to speak of Amelia's birth, and it struck fear into the depths of my heart. It is a fear I now share with you, for I sense that the darkness that surrounds Lawrence is a perilous one. I implore you to be vigilant, to protect your dear Amelia with all the strength that a mother's love can muster.

Amelia's true lineage and the identity of her father, Lawrence, are secrets best left in the shadows. It is with a heavy heart that I utter these words, but I believe it is for the safety and well-being of your precious child. Keep her hidden, my dear friend, and be cautious in the presence of Lawrence or his emissaries. Trust your instincts, for they are a mother's most potent weapon.

Enclosed with this letter is a gift for Amelia. It isn't from me, but from Lawrence - a token afterthought he wanted me to give you to acknowledge Amelia's birth. I must stress that it was given with more disgust than feeling. However, I believe it could be a beautiful symbol of your love for Amelia, if given with that intent. It's a golden locket in a velvet box. Please save it for Amelia and give it to her at the right time. Let her know that it's a symbol of your love as her mother, something to treasure and keep close to her heart always.

In closing, my dear Allison, I wish for you and Amelia the love and happiness that you so richly deserve. Your strength and resilience inspire me, and I hold you both close in my thoughts and prayers. I hope that our paths may cross again, and that the weight of this burden may someday be lifted. Until then,

> *remember that my heart is with you, and that you are never truly alone.*
>
> *With all the love in my heart,*
>
> *Alba Weston*

"This letter... it's incredible," I said, my voice barely more than a whisper. "It's written proof that Laine is Amelia's father. And it even warns that he might want to harm them."

"It's pretty damning to say the least. Everything's in there... identity, motive, threats." Chris paused and looked at the letter again. "Alba risked a lot to write this, so her fear for their safety was real."

"Why did she send the locket?" I wondered out loud. "She wrote that it was nothing more than a token afterthought."

"Read how she worded that sentence in the letter," Chris responded. "A gift for Amelia to acknowledge her birth. Lawrence gave Alba the locket to give to Amelia... it tied him to her in a tangible way."

I read the next sentences of the letter out loud.

I believe it could be a beautiful symbol of your love for Amelia, if given with that intent. It's a golden locket in a velvet box. Please save it for Amelia and give it to her at the right time.

"Interesting how she worded that. What did she mean by telling Allison to give it to her *'at the right time*?'"

Chris studied the letter, then turned away, deep

in thought. "Maybe it's what she didn't write that's important." He turned back and our eyes locked. "At some point, Amelia was going to want to know who her father was. I think Alba thought revealing that Laine was her father would be the right time to give her the gift."

"And to let her know she was loved very much."

"A symbol of Allison's love, yes. I think Laine carried out his threats, leading to their disappearance, and I think Amelia's remains are still here."

"You think she's in the well, don't you," I breathed, my eyes never leaving his.

"I do." he replied, before turning away. "We need to pay another visit to George Benningly Jr. and show him the letter."

"What would you hope to accomplish with another visit to that disgusting excuse for a human being?" I asked, folding the letter carefully. "He'd probably just blow it off as another one of our schemes to cash in, and I doubt he would care anything about Laine being Amelia's father."

"I'll tell him I'm going to dig up the well." Chris turned to me with a determined look. "If we find Amelia's remains, we put her to rest, and Benningly won't have anything else to say about it."

"That's going to be an interesting conversation."

I glanced down at Maddie. Her chest was rising and falling peacefully as she slept. We sat there, enveloped by the silence and warmth of the room, and a puzzled look appeared on Chris's face.

"You know, it just hit me—I haven't heard a peep from Norman or Kat since the whole snake show in the barn.

We should go make sure they're okay."

"We should," I nodded, feeling a twinge of concern.

Chris led the way as we headed through the kitchen and out the back door. The late afternoon sun cast long shadows across the yard as we made our way around the side of the house. To our surprise, we found Kat standing over Norman's prone body near the back of the van. His jacket was scorched and smoking, evidence of a recent encounter with the electric fence he had constructed. In his haste to escape the snake, Norman had forgotten about his own creation, and had been 'clotheslined' as he sought safety in the van.

"Dumb shit," Kat muttered, shaking her head in disbelief. She took a deep swig from the wine bottle she held, clearly unconcerned by Norman's predicament.

"Is he okay?" I asked.

"His pride will be hurt more than anything else," Chris replied with a smile. "I think he'll live."

I couldn't help but let out a small, relieved chuckle. Despite the chaos that surrounded us, moments like these reminded me of how much I loved this crazy group.

Chapter Thirteen

Angel

June 3rd, 1961

The low hanging clouds partially hid the sun, creating patchy shadows that spread across the wooded trail. Angel's long brown hair flowed behind her like a silken banner as she guided her horse, Ice, along the familiar path. Her eyes, a piercing blue, scanned her surroundings with curiosity and confidence. At eighteen years of age, she was an image of striking beauty and poise, no doubt influenced by her privileged upbringing as the daughter of Lawrence and Julia Laine.

The rhythmic beat of her gray stallion's hooves provided a soothing background for her thoughts. The woods around her were alive with the sounds of birds and rustling leaves, a symphony of nature's beauty. It was moments like these that Angel cherished: the freedom and connection to the world around her, and the vast estate she called home.

Angel rode up to an old wooden fence just off the trail, and a flash of movement caught her eye. A little girl, no older than ten, was playing in the pasture. Curious, Angel steered Ice closer, the gray stallion's hooves thudding softly on the damp earth. The child glanced up and noticed Angel, her eyes wide at the sight of the beautiful young woman astride the magnificent gray horse.

"Hey there," Angel called out, her voice lilting and friendly. "I'm Angel. What's your name?"

The girl froze, her eyes nervously darting back and forth between Angel and the open field around her. After a moment she spoke, her voice quiet and airy.

"Amelia."

"Amelia," Angel repeated, flashing a warm smile. "Nice to meet you. What are you doing all the way out here?"

"Playing," Amelia replied softly, "I live here."

"No way." Angel perked up with curiosity. "You live in that farmhouse over there?" Amelia nodded, her eyes never leaving the beautiful gray horse.

"Whoa, I had no clue someone was living this close to our estate," Angel said, looking closer at Amelia. The girl was dressed kinda cute, but you could tell she didn't come from money.

"Wanna come see my horse?" Angel asked, as she carefully slid off the saddle to stand at the fence's edge. "There's nothing to worry about, he's friendly." Amelia hesitated for a moment before cautiously approaching.

"Been in that farmhouse long?" Angel asked casually, genuinely curious about the mysterious girl.

"Yeah, my whole life... with my mama."

Angel's gaze shifted to the old building and back to Amelia, trying to guess the young girl's age. "What grade are you in school?"

"School?" Amelia asked, with a confused expression.

"I've never been to school. Mama says it's not safe for me."

"Sounds lonely," Angel lamented. "Do you have any friends to play with?"

"No," the young girl admitted, her voice breaking slightly.

"Wanna be friends?" Angel asked gently. The idea of a kid living all alone kinda pulled at her heartstrings.

"Okay," Amelia agreed, looking up with wide, hopeful eyes.

"What about your family," Angel pressed, trying to get more information. "Just you and your mom?"

"Uh-huh," Amelia nodded. "Just us. I don't have a dad... well, I don't know him."

"That must be hard for you. My old man's known by everyone," Angel giggled, proudly. A hint of sadness slipped into her voice as she continued. "I can't wrap my head around someone not ever knowing their dad."

The clouds parted for a moment allowing sunlight to glint off the gray stallion's coat, casting a dazzling shimmer in Amelia's wide eyes. She couldn't help but stare at the magnificent creature, feeling as if she were in the presence of something truly magical.

"His name is Ice," Angel said, stroking the horse's powerful neck. "You've seen a horse before, haven't you?"

"Only in pictures," Amelia replied, her voice bolder now.

"You wanna pet him? He's got a really soft nose... feel it."

With trembling hands, Amelia reached out and gently touched the velvety softness of Ice's nose. The warmth of the horse's breath tickled her fingers, making her smile. "Oh wow," she breathed, her eyes shining with wonder.

"See? I told you he was friendly."

Amelia continued caressing Ice's nose, and noticed a blue ribbon pinned to the blanket under his saddle. "What's that for?" she asked, curiously.

Angel smiled proudly. "That's a ribbon I won at a show-jumping competition. I have tons of 'em, but I thought Ice deserved to feel special today, so I pinned it on him."

"You must be a really good rider."

"I do ok," Angel replied, her cheeks coloring slightly. "Here," she said, as she unpinned the ribbon and handed it to Amelia. "I want you to have it."

Amelia's face lit up as she took the ribbon from Angel's outstretched hand. "This is the nicest thing anyone has ever given me."

"Glad I can give you a piece of my world. Besides, everyone needs to feel special."

Angel felt warm inside seeing the girl's broad smile. A moment passed before she spoke again, an idea fresh in her mind. "There's a competition coming up at my place in a couple of weeks. I'd love for you to come and watch me jump."

"Really?" Amelia asked, her eyes wide.

"Yes, really, and if I win a ribbon I'll give it to you, I promise."

Amelia bit her lip, uncertain. "I don't know if mama will let me go, but I can ask."

"Ask her," Angel said with a smile. "And I'll tell my mom to make *sure* you're there. I know she'll want to meet you."

"Thanks," Amelia whispered, touched by her new friend's kindness.

"Wanna go on a short ride with me?"

"Me?" Amelia stuttered, eyeing the awesome gray stallion.

"Heck yeah, you," Angel shot back. "You can hop on behind me. I want you to get the feel of it."

Amelia's eyes widened and she nodded eagerly. With practiced elegance, Angel mounted Ice and reached out her hand, helping the young girl up and into the space behind her. Amelia marveled at the sensation of being on a horse for the first time. The warmth of Ice's body beneath her and the smell of his well-groomed coat seemed to envelop her. It was a world entirely different from any she'd ever known.

"Ready?" Angel asked, turning her head slightly to look back.

"Ready," Amelia confirmed, her voice trembling with excitement.

With a gentle nudge, Ice began to slowly walk, each step deliberate and powerful. Amelia held on tightly, her knuckles white, as the unfamiliar motion of the horse's gait rocked her body gently back and forth. A mixture of exhilaration and disbelief flooded her senses as they glided effortlessly across the pasture.

"What do you think?"

"It's so different... like a dream," Amelia sighed, her grip around Angel's waist relaxing. Angel felt different, too... something about this girl struck a chord deep inside her. She felt a connection that she didn't quite understand.

Angel guided Ice to a gentle stop near the fence where they first met. Reluctantly, Amelia dismounted.

"Hey," Angel said, locking eyes with Amelia. "You gotta be at the horse show, okay? Promise me you'll show up."

"I promise," Amelia replied with a determined voice. "I'll be there."

With a final wave, Angel coaxed Ice into a graceful canter, her figure retreating into the woods. Amelia stood watching until they disappeared, clutching the blue ribbon tightly in her hand.

※

Angel arrived at the main stable, dismounting from *Ice* with a graceful ease that betrayed her years of practice. A groom appeared, seemingly from nowhere, and took the reins from her hands, leading the horse inside for a well-deserved rest. Angel could hardly contain her excitement as she approached her mother, Julia, who sat in a chair near the stable office, sipping tea.

"Did you have a nice ride?" Julia asked curiously.

"Mom, I met the most amazing girl," Angel gushed, her words tumbling out in a torrent of excitement. "Her name is Amelia, and she's never been to school or had any friends. I invited her to the show here at the estate. I hope that's okay."

Julia's expression remained warm as she sat down her tea and rose from the chair to take Angel's riding gloves and helmet. "Of course, it's fine. I'm glad you made a new friend, and I look forward to meeting her."

"Amelia is such a sweet girl, but she seems so shy and

sheltered," Angel confided in Julia as they walked toward the main residence. "She told me she's spent her whole life at that old farmhouse on the edge of our estate."

Julia raised an eyebrow, surprised. "Really? I never knew anyone lived there."

The scent of blooming roses wafted through the air, mingling with the distant aroma of horses as Angel and Julia entered the doors off the veranda. Lawrence was standing near the Great Room fireplace, his ever-present glass of bourbon securely in hand. Julia's eyes narrowed at the sight, her lips tightening into a thin line.

"Why are you drinking this early in the day?"

Lawrence took a slow sip from his glass, savoring the taste before answering dismissively, "Early for who? I've been working for hours, dear, stressing over phone calls. I just needed something to take the edge off."

"Your mornings wouldn't be so stressful if you didn't drink so much," Julia retorted, but her words seemed to have little impact.

Angel watched the exchange, biting her lip and feeling a pang of discomfort. The tension between her parents was palpable, but she couldn't bring herself to intervene. Instead, she tried to steer the conversation to a new topic, hoping to distract them from their brewing argument.

"Dad, I met a girl today on my ride."

"Is that so?" Lawrence replied, his gaze flicking toward her briefly before returning to Julia. His indifference made Angel's heart sink, but she persisted.

"Yeah, and I invited her to the jumper show we're hosting," she said, injecting as much enthusiasm into her words as she could muster.

"Very nice," he said, draining the last of his bourbon with a final, deliberate swallow. "I'm sure it'll be quite the event."

The conversation seemed to end there, leaving Angel frustrated and Julia discouraged.

"I'm going upstairs to get a bath." Angel said finally. She looked at her mom, rolled her eyes and mouthed a silent message that indicated she wanted the topic dropped. Without speaking, she spun on her heel and took the grand stairs two at a time, bounding up to her room.

Julia took a deep breath, gathering her thoughts before addressing Lawrence further. She could sense a storm brewing beneath the surface, and she knew it was time to confront it head-on.

"Lawrence," Julia began, her voice steady but laced with suspicion, "Angel told you about meeting someone today... a little girl named Amelia. She said she's living at the farmhouse. Did you know someone was living there?"

At the mention of Amelia's name, Lawrence's eyes widened ever so slightly, betraying a flicker of shock that he quickly tried to mask. Julia didn't miss this change in his demeanor. The atmosphere in the room grew tense.

"I don't know anything about that," he replied, his words slurred from the bourbon he'd nursed for far too long.

"Really, Lawrence?" Julia asked, her voice firm. "Your reaction suggests otherwise. What do you know about this strange little girl living in our farmhouse?"

Lawrence's face turned pale. "If anyones living there, it must be someone George knows."

"George? You're best friend George?" Julia raised an

eyebrow, her suspicions growing stronger. "Why would George have anything to do with it? And why would he have people living in our farmhouse without telling us?"

"Because it's none of our business," Lawrence snapped, his cheeks flushing with anger, or perhaps something else. He set his empty glass on the mantel with a sharp clink. "The property was deeded to him years ago, Julia. It's probably just some relatives or close friends of his."

"Still, we should at least know who's living on our estate," Julia insisted, refusing to let the matter go. Her instincts were telling her that there was more to this story than was being told.

"Fine. I'll speak to George about it!" Lawrence's voice was raised, and his words seemed final. It was obvious he wanted nothing more than to put an end to the conversation. His abrupt dismissal only served to heighten Julia's unease.

"Please do," she replied, her voice firm. Her gaze locked with Lawrence's, and she couldn't help but wonder what secrets lay hidden behind his dark eyes.

"Speaking of Amelia," Julia countered, her tone taking on a more sarcastic edge than she'd intended, "Angel just told you she invited her to the July 4th Jumpers show. Will, you make sure George extends the invitation to her family when you speak with him. I would think he knows them well enough since they're staying at *his* place."

"Of course," Lawrence said with a sigh, his eyes darting away from Julia's piercing gaze. "As I said, I'll speak with him."

Julia studied her husband for a moment longer before

deciding to let the matter rest... for now.

"Alright, then," she said, her voice firm yet tinged with a weariness that echoed through her bones. "I'll leave you to your... drinking." With that, she pivoted and exited the room, her footsteps echoing in the tense silence that lingered.

"Mrs. Laine?" a servant called as she passed. "Can I assist you?"

"Please accompany me to my bedroom," Julia requested, not breaking stride. The servant quickly fell into step behind her as they ascended the grand staircase, the plush carpet beneath their feet doing little to muffle the thoughts swirling in Julia's mind. She paused at the top, glancing down at Lawrence. She wanted to believe he would be honest with her, but the gnawing doubt in the pit of her stomach told her otherwise.

"Is everything alright, Mrs. Laine?" the servant asked.

"Everything's fine," Julia replied curtly, forcing a tight-lipped smile.

Lawrence Laine wasted no time in retreating to his office, the heavy oak door offering a semblance of sanctuary as he closed it behind him. The faint sound of Julia's retreating footsteps had barely faded before he snatched up the telephone from its cradle, his fingers drumming impatiently on the polished surface of his mahogany desk.

"Get me Benningly, *now!*" Laine barked into the receiver, his voice shaking with barely concealed agitation. Within minutes, George had been located backstage and picked up the call.

FIREFLIES

"Lawrence, to what do I owe the pleasure?", he greeted Laine, a hint of exasperation in his voice. He was in New York, dealing with the fallout from Lawrence's latest misadventures. "Before you start, I must warn you... you're not going to like what I have to say. Sponsors are getting cold feet. They want to pay less for commercials since your ratings are down."

"Damn the show, George!" Lawrence spat, his grip tightening around the phone. The harsh reality of his dwindling success stung like a slap in the face, but it was only one of many issues that plagued him. "I've got bigger problems here."

"Alright, calm down," George said, trying to mollify his old friend. "What could be more important than losing your career?"

Laine was momentarily stunned, his mind muddled by the alcohol he had consumed. "What the hell are you talking about?" Laine responded, his slurred speech belying his confusion. "I have the best show on television, and everyone knows it," he added, with a note of defiance.

"Your personal life is affecting the show, Lawrence," George replied bluntly. "Popular guest stars are dropping out left and right, joining other shows. Your drinking has become a serious problem, and your skirt chasing isn't helping either. The tabloids are having a field day with your exploits. If you don't pull yourself together, this could be the end."

"You're right... this may be the end, George." Laine replied in a somber tone.

"Go on," George replied cautiously, sensing the urgency

in his old friend's voice.

"Angel, my daughter, met a young girl today when she was out riding. She said her name was Amelia."

"Amelia?" George hesitated for a moment, weighing his words carefully. "This could be bad... really bad."

"Amelia was invited to the estate by Angel," Lawrence continued, his voice strained. "Julia insists that she attend an event happening here in a few weeks. You know that can't happen. You need to make sure Amelia and Allison don't set foot on this property... ever."

"Lawrence, your personal life is spiraling out of control."

"Damn it, George," Lawrence hissed, his bloodshot eyes narrowing in frustration. "I don't have time for your lectures. Fix this George... just do what i fucking ask."

"Alright, alright," George sighed, relenting under the weight of Lawrence's desperation. "I'll see what I can do."

Laine hung up the phone and sank into his chair, fingers drumming on the desk as he stared blankly at the wall. The ticking of the ornate clock on his desk seemed to echo through the room, each second a reminder of the precarious web of secrets that threatened to unravel his life.

"Angel," he whispered. "What have you done?"

»» •◆• ««

A few days later, George found himself standing on the doorstep of the old farmhouse at the edge of Laine's estate. It had been years since he had last seen the girl, and the thought of facing her mother, Allison, filled him with unease.

Allison answered at his knock, her eyes guarded as she took in his presence. "George. What are you doing here?" she asked, her tone icy.

"Amelia told you about the invitation, didn't she?" George inquired, cutting straight to the point. Allison's gaze hardened, and she crossed her arms defensively.

"Angel Laine invited my daughter to their estate," she confirmed, defiance sparking in her eyes. "And I'm inclined to accept the invitation. Amelia wants to go, and I'm tired of telling her no to everything she asks for without explanation."

"It's not a good idea for you and Amelia to attend the event at the estate. You know there will be questions, things asked that I doubt you'll be prepared to answer."

"Like where the hell is Amelia's father?" Allison shot back, turning quickly to face George now standing just inside the doorway. "Imagine the looks on everyone's faces when I spill the beans... that Lawrence stashed me away here years ago to keep the lid on our little secret affair and the child it created." Allison took a step closer, her fists clenched into angry balls. "I haven't laid eyes on Lawrence in 9 years, not a peep from him, not a letter or a ring on the phone. He doesn't give a damn about us, so why the hell should we give a damn about him and his charmed life." Allison's eyes were brimming with tears of anger and rage as she pushed even closer. "I think it's high time everyone finds out who Amelia's father is."

"Lawrence will never allow that," George warned, his

voice firm but not unkind.

"Allow?" Allison echoed, her fury dominating as she began to march back and forth. She started to laugh - and cry at the same time. "Allow... oh my God!" she screamed before returning to stand inches from George's face. "It's time, George... it's time! Amelia deserves something better than this shitty life of being hidden away, cut off from everything and everyone!"

Allison looked away from George, surprised by her own words. A bitterness filled her, and her voice was tinged with resentment. "Angel rode in here in all her glory... decked out in her expensive riding gear. Amelia thought she was some creature from another world... and frankly, she is. She's from a world Amelia's never known, and I think it's time she gets a piece of that world. She deserves the same wealth and privilege as Lawrence's other children."

"Allison, it will never happen," he stated emphatically. "You can't reveal Lawrence's secret. It would destroy him."

"*Then maybe he deserves to be destroyed*," Allison fired back, her voice trembling. "This event, horse show, whatever it is would be the perfect time to reveal the truth about Lawrence and Amelia --"

"Think about what you're saying," George interrupted, his voice cold. "If you pursue this plan, the money will disappear. You and Amelia will be left with nothing."

Allison hesitated, her resolve wavering, but the fire in her eyes remained undimmed. "I'll do whatever it takes to give my daughter the life she deserves," she spat fiercely. "And you can't stop me."

Reluctantly, George nodded and walked out the open

door, anxious to defuse the confrontation. Maybe with time Allison would change her mind... this was all he could hope for. He glanced back at the farmhouse as he drove out the gate, noticing a small figure peeping from behind the open doorframe. "Amelia." he sighed, feeling an unfamiliar heaviness in his chest. His doubts grew as he headed towards the Laine estate, convinced that the precarious balance they had held for so long was about to end.

George found Lawrence in his office, slumped over his desk with an empty glass in one hand and a bottle of bourbon in the other. The room reeked of alcohol and regret.

"Lawrence, we need to talk," George began cautiously.

"Damn it, George!" Lawrence slurred, slamming his glass down on the desk, "You better have nothing but good things to say to me. I told you to fix this!"

"Believe me, I tried," George replied, exasperation dripping from his words. "Allison is determined to reveal the truth about Amelia. She wouldn't listen to reason."

"Then I'll deal with her myself," Lawrence growled, wiping his mouth with the back of his hand. His eyes were bloodshot and unfocused, but still held a spark of determination.

"Lawrence, you're in no state to handle anything," George cautioned. "Don't do something you'll regret... think... please."

"*Get out!*" Lawrence roared, hurling the empty glass at George. It shattered into a thousand pieces beside him, mirroring the fractured lives of everyone involved. George left the office, feeling that the storm they had all been dreading was about arrive, and there would be no shelter from its fury.

CHAPTER FOURTEEN

DO YOU HAVE LINK SAUSAGE?

"Alright, turn here," I said, eyes glued to my phone. Chris guided the truck into the narrow entrance off Loudoun Street, and my eyes widened in disbelief. "Fire Station One? Seriously? What is it with this historical society and fire stations?"

Chris couldn't help but chuckle, remembering our first meeting with George Benningly Jr. at the museum downtown.

"What... what's so funny?" I asked, curiously.

"Just recalling our last 'fun-filled' meeting with George." Chris replied, peeking over at me expecting a response.

"Ah, King George on his wheelchair throne," I muttered under my breath, recalling the man's pious personality that fit the image all too well. The thought of facing that rude S.O.B. again made my stomach twist with anxiety. "Still doesn't explain why we're pulling up to a fire station."

"The historical society is hosting their annual Heritage Breakfast here... it's a big fundraiser event. I'm sure George will be inside." Chris threw the truck into park and turned off the engine. "Our presence will be a surprise for George, and I doubt he'll be pleased to see us."

"Good, because I'm not exactly thrilled to see him either," I replied, crossing my arms.

As we climbed the stairs to the second floor 'Blaze' community room, the smell of breakfast hit me like a warm blanket on a cold morning. The room was abuzz with chatter and clanking dishes, while sunlight spilled through the tall windows, casting long shadows on the linoleum floor.

"Wow, this is quite the event," I remarked, eyeing the banquet hall adorned with festive decorations.

"Yep, they don't hold back for their Heritage Breakfast," Chris replied, grinning.

The room was filled with circular tables, each set with crisp white tablecloths and gleaming silverware. People were gathered around them, laughing, and enjoying their breakfast. Along the walls of the room, several more people huddled together, admiring historical pictures from Loudoun County that had been procured from various museums for the occasion. Each image seemed to tell its own rich story, emphasizing the importance of the historical society to the community.

"Smells amazing in here," I said, my eyes lighting up as I took in the large buffet spread at the back of the room. "Why am I suddenly starving?"

"I could use a bite myself," Chris agreed, watching as eager attendees moved through the line, filling their plates with steaming pancakes, scrambled eggs, and sausage before returning to their seats to savor the feast.

"Ok, Sam, keep a lid on it," Chris whispered as we walked

further into the bustling room, "we're here for answers, not sausage and eggs."

"Speak for yourself," I joked, my nostrils flaring as I caught a whiff of freshly brewed coffee.

"Looks like we've found our man," Chris whispered, nodding toward George Benningly Jr., who had stationed himself behind the buffet table. He was seated in his motorized wheelchair, barking orders at others on how to fill the plates, ever the king in control of his kingdom.

I raised an eyebrow and sighed. "Let's get this over with."

As we approached, George's eyes flicked up to meet ours, and his expression immediately soured. "Ah, if it isn't our paranormal investigators," George said with a sneer as we approached. "What are you two doing here?" he asked snidely. "Surely you're not here to support the society?"

"Hello, George," Chris greeted him warmly, unfazed by his disdain. "Actually, we've always supported the efforts of the historical society, and today is no exception." Chris glanced at me before continuing, "In fact, we're planning on making a generous donation in return for a nice breakfast."

"Is that so?" George replied skeptically, giving me a disgusted look which I promptly returned.

"Absolutely," Chris said, his voice steady and sincere. "We believe in the work the society does, and we're happy to contribute."

"Is that all you're here for?" George asked, doubt evident in his voice.

"Actually, no," Chris admitted. "We were hoping to have a moment of your time to discuss something important."

"I assume your desire to speak with me has little to do with history and everything to do with ghosts, am I right?" George spat and rolled his eyes. "More paranormal nonsense about that farmhouse I presume?"

"No, this is different," Chris insisted, glancing at me for support. "We have new information, concrete evidence about what happened to Allison and Amelia Luce."

"Really... evidence?" George's tone was dripping with sarcasm, but he seemed to recognize the gravity of Chris's words. He silenced him with a quick gesture, not wanting others to overhear the conversation, and wheeled himself from behind the buffet to a quieter part of the room. As we followed, a couple of women attendees stopped Chris briefly, big smiles stretched across their faces. "We're so glad you're here," one of them said, batting her eyelashes. "We can't wait for your next ghost tour!"

I bristled, knowing the women were flirting. Chris gave me a look, silently urging me to bite my tongue as he politely thanked the women and moved along. Benningly, having witnessed the exchange, was not amused.

"Enough with your groupies," George admonished Chris when we reached a secluded corner. "Show me this 'concrete evidence' you speak-of and make it quick. I'm needed on the buffet line."

"Actually," I interjected, looking around the room, "it seems like your workers are doing better without you there to direct them."

"Samantha," George snapped, narrowing his eyes. "You're much more attractive when your mouth isn't open."

"Alright, George," Chris said calmly, cutting off my

impending angry reply. "We found a letter at the farmhouse. It was used as a bookmark in an old book Amelia owned."

"Ha!" George exclaimed, his eyes betraying his skepticism. "And how do you know this book belonged to Amelia? Let me guess: more ghost hunting nonsense?"

"Actually, yes," Chris replied, unfazed by George's mockery. "Our investigations and interactions with Amelia's spirit led us to it. Now, if you'd let me finish..."

George rolled his eyes but didn't interrupt, clearly itching to escape our presence.

"You might want to sit down for this, George. Oh, wait--" I quipped before Chris shot me a warning glance. I couldn't resist getting in one more dig.

"The letter was addressed to Amelia's mother, Allison," Chris continued, watching George's expression carefully. "It warned her never to reveal that Lawrence Laine was Amelia's father."

George's eyes widened, and for a moment, his bluster seemed to deflate. "That's impossible," he sputtered. "What makes you think I'd believe such nonsense?"

"Because we have the letter," Chris replied, his voice steady. "And we believe that Laine was involved in their disappearance."

For a moment, George's face registered shock before it twisted into anger. "So, I was right all along!" he spat. "This is just some ruse to make money off the Laine Estate!"

"George, we have no desire to gain anything but the truth about Allison and Amelia's disappearances," Chris insisted, his voice firm and sincere.

"Produce the letter, then!" George challenged, his face red with anger. "Show me this so-called evidence and let me take it to the director of the Laine Foundation! She'll know what to do with your 'concrete evidence.'"

"Actually," Chris replied, trying his best to appear calm, "I think it's best if I contact the director myself. That is, once Amelia's remains are recovered."

"Amelia's remains?" George sputtered, his eyes widening in shock. "Are you suggesting that her body is hidden somewhere on the property?"

"Hidden might not be the right word," Chris said carefully, aware that we were treading on delicate ground. "But, yes, I believe Amelia's remains will be found there. Specifically, I think they're in the well."

"Preposterous!" George exclaimed, his face turning red. "You'll need more than a piece of paper to convince me or anyone else that Laine is Amelia's father, much less responsible for her death!"

"Maybe so," I chimed in, "but we're going to find out the truth, even if that means digging up the old well on the farmhouse property."

"You'll do no such thing!" George thundered, drawing the attention of several nearby guests. He lowered his voice and continued, "That property is under my protection, and I won't have it defiled by your paranormal nonsense!"

"George," Chris continued, trying to keep his voice steady, "We're not asking for permission to dig up the well, we're telling you of our intentions... we're digging it up."

"Absolutely not!" Benningly roared, his face turning an alarming shade of red as he glared at Chris. "You have

FIREFLIES

no right to deface my property! I will call the Laine Foundation director myself and have you and Samantha's little family removed from the premises immediately!"

His outburst was so loud that the chatter and clinking of silverware in the room came to a sudden halt. Heads turned our way, curious eyes boring into us. George seemed to realize that he had drawn unwanted attention and quickly regained his composure.

"Please, everyone," he said, forcing a tight smile. "This is just a minor disagreement. Continue enjoying your meal."

He fumbled in his pocket for his cell phone, his hands shaking with barely restrained anger. Once he found it, he dialed a number with purpose, his eyes never leaving Chris's face.

"Madam Director," he began, his voice dripping with false politeness. "I apologize for disturbing you, but there's a matter of utmost urgency that needs your attention. Chris Janey and Samantha Payne are here with me, and they're planning to dig up the well on the farmhouse property."

He paused, listening to the director's response. I took Chris's hand and held it, seeking reassurance.

"Chris is a paranormal hack who's attempting to concoct a story to smear the Laine Foundation," George continued, his words twisted with disdain. "I believe it's in our best interest to have them removed from the property immediately."

Though we couldn't hear the director's response, it was clear that something she said had surprised George. His face paled, and his grip on the phone tightened. For a few tense moments, he listened, only offering short replies.

"Y-yes, Madam Director... Of course... I understand. Yes, ma'am... she's right here," George's tone was a mixture of annoyance and begrudging respect. He handed me the phone with a tight-lipped smile, his eyes filled with curiosity as to why the director emeritus wanted to speak with me directly.

"Hello, this is Samantha," I spoke into the phone, my heart pounding.

The voice on the other end was that of an elderly woman, her eloquence and grace shining through despite her advanced age. "Ah, Samantha," the director replied, her voice like velvet. "I apologize for the insults. It seems that my dear friend George can be quite... passionate about matters concerning the Laine Foundation."

"Understandably so, ma'am," I replied, glancing at George, who was glaring at me. "And I apologize as well. We didn't mean to cause you any concern."

"It's not a problem, Samantha, I trust your intentions are sincere. I gather that you and Mr. Janney have been investigating the farmhouse, and have found something interesting?" Her tone warm yet authoritative. "Is this about Amelia and Allison?"

"Yes, Madam Director," I said with conviction. "Chris's paranormal investigations have indeed revealed evidence that relates to the disappearances, and Amelia's spirit has appeared numerous times to us. My daughter, Maddie, has become quite close with her."

"Your daughter Maddie is ill, isn't she?" the director inquired.

"Yes, that's right," I replied, trying to keep my voice

steady. "How did you know about that?"

"I'm responsible for granting your stay at the farmhouse," the director said, her voice growing soft. "Your editor-in-chief, Author Jameson, is a dear friend. He wrote to request the stay on your behalf and told of your daughter's situation. It reminded me of Allison and Amelia." The elderly woman seemed to pause and reflect for a moment before continuing. "Nobody has been in that house since they disappeared," she said eventually. "It just felt right to have a young mother and daughter living there again, even if it was only for a little while."

I fought back tears, my voice trembling. "I'm so grateful to you for letting me and Maddie stay there..." I said quietly. "I will never forget your kindness and please, call me Sam."

"All right, Sam," the director continued. "Tell me what it is that you and Mr. Janney want to do at the farmhouse?"

"We want to dig up the well on the property because we believe Amelia's remains are there." I whispered, glancing at Chris for reassurance.

"And what led you to this conclusion?" the director inquired after a brief silence.

"We found a letter in an old book, one that belonged to Amelia," I explained. "The letter was from Alba Weston, warning Allison to keep quiet about Amelia being Laine's daughter. The implications were clear, they were in danger, and Amelia's spirit often appears at the well."

"Are you still in possession of this letter?" the director asked.

"Yes, we are," I replied firmly.

The director's soft words seemed to hold a tinge of

sadness as she spoke, "Please tell Maddie that I hope she gets better soon, and give her my love, would you?" After a brief pause, she continued, "Let me have a word with Mr. Janney, please."

I quickly passed the phone to Chris over George's expectant, outstretched hand. His confusion was evident as I told Chris that the director wanted to speak with him.

"I must apologize for any inconvenience this call may have caused you --" Chris's comment was cut short as he was obviously interrupted by the director words.

"Of course, Madam Director," he replied, doing his best to sound composed. "We only want to reveal the truth about Amelia and Allison's disappearance. I assure you, we have no intention of causing any harm to you or the foundation."

When the elderly woman continued speaking, Chris's countenance quickly shifted into one of complete shock. His complexion paled and his eyes widened in disbelief.

"I... I look forward to possibly meeting you one day," Chris stammered, "We'll do everything in our power to honor your wishes." He fixed his gaze on me, wide-eyed and evidently surprised by something that had been said. "Thank you, ma'am, I will," he confirmed with a final nod before handing the phone to George. "She wants to talk to you."

"Fine," George growled, snatching the phone from Chris. "Madam Director, I assure you that Samantha and Maddie will be removed from the property as soon as possible. I --" He paused as the director interrupted him, his face turning crimson with each word she spoke.

"Yes, Madam Director...yes...yes." His voice diminished with every word, and it became clear that things weren't going according to plan.

"Very well," George said through gritted teeth before ending the call. He glared at Chris, clearly displeased with the outcome. "The director has instructed me not to interfere with your plans to dig up the well," he said reluctantly. "It seems you have her permission."

"Thank you, George," Chris replied, trying to hide his satisfaction.

Perplexed and angry, George shook his head. "Now, if you'll excuse me, I have work to attend to." He gestured towards the food table, itching to return to his role as king of the buffet.

"Do you have link sausage over there?" Chris asked, much to George's annoyance. "I really love link sausage."

"Get in line," he snapped, rolling his eyes as he motored away.

"Thank you, George," I said mockingly, offering a final sarcastic smile.

Sunlight reflected off the truck's windshield as we stepped out of the fire station, leaving behind the clatter of dishes and laughter of the crowd. I could still taste the sweetness of maple syrup on my tongue, the morning feast now a memory. Chris rubbed his hands together, the crisp autumn air making him shiver slightly.

"Okay, Chris," I said, my eyes searching his, "You can't keep me in suspense any longer. What happened during that phone call? What did she say that made you freak out?"

Chris leaned against the truck, feeling its warmth seep in through his clothes. The parking lot was alive with the sound of birdsong and rustling leaves, creating a peaceful backdrop to our conversation.

"First of all," he began, watching my reaction closely, "The director emeritus is very interested in our encounters with Amelia. She encouraged us to continue our investigation."

"I thought that too from my conversation with her," I smiled in agreement. "So, she believes we've had encounters with Amelia's spirit?"

"Seems like it," Chris replied, nodding. "But there's more, something I didn't expect."

"Go on," I urged, my patience pushed to its limits.

"The letter we found in the book...the warning to Allison." He paused for effect, letting the words sink in. "The director emeritus told me that she wrote it."

"Wait, what?" my eyes widened, my hand flying to cover my mouth. "You mean she's --"

"Exactly," Chris interrupted, watching the realization spread across my face. "Alba Weston is the Director Emeritus of the Laine Foundation."

Chapter Fifteen

Time to Dig

Beads of sweat formed on Chris and Norman's foreheads as they unloaded the truck. A wheelbarrow's metal frame clanged against the ground as it was offloaded, followed by the dull thud of shovels and a pickaxe. Bags filled with cement and gravel were stacked nearby, ready to shore up the loose sides of the well if needed.

"Are we gonna need all this stuff?" Norman asked, wiping the sweat from his brow with the back of his hand.

"Yeah, it might be a bit much, but I'd rather be ready," Chris said, throwing a garden hose over his shoulder. "Who knows what we'll come across down there, you know?"

"Can't believe we're actually going through with this," Norman said, pushing his glasses up the bridge of his nose. His lanky form leaned against the truck, seeking a momentary reprieve from the effort.

"Me neither, but we got the permission to dig so we're going to dig."

Norman nodded solemnly, understanding the gravity of their mission.

"Once we get everything unloaded, I want you to set up a perimeter fence around the well," Chris instructed, nodding toward the pile of electric fence remains nearby. "Got to keep our dig site secure and private."

"Should I electrify it like before?" Norman asked, a playful glint in his eyes.

"Let's see, mud, water, metal tools... what do you think?"

"Right, not a good idea," Norman conceded, rubbing the back of his neck sheepishly. "Sorry, I haven't been myself since that little shock yesterday."

Chris laughed, giving Norman a friendly pat on the back. "No worries, my friend. We live, and learn, right?"

"Sometimes the hard way," Norman added, a twinkle in his eyes betraying his embarrassment.

"Let's set up cameras and lighting around the well," Chris said, his voice steady and focused. "We need to document everything, for personal *and* legal reasons.

"I can make that happen," Norman replied, already mentally cataloguing what equipment they had in the van that was still functional. He looked around, noting the dwindling sunlight. "When are you planning to start the dig?"

"As soon as everything's set up. We need to move quickly before someone has a change of heart and tries to stop us."

"Right," Norman agreed, removing his gloves. "Do you really think we'll find Amelia's remains down there?"

Chris paused, leaning on a shovel. His eyes seemed to bore into the ground beneath them, as if willing it to reveal its secrets. "I hope so, Norman. For everyone's sake."

The vibration of Chris's phone startled him. He quickly

grabbed it and noticed a message from Samantha flashing on the screen:

> Hey Chris, I'm upstairs with Maddie. She's not doing well. Kat is here with me to help. I don't want to leave her alone.

The sun was casting its warm golden light over the field as Chris stood, his thumb hovering over the screen of his phone. He blinked back the sting of emotion, taking a deep breath before texting Sam back.

> I'm sorry to hear that. Is there anything I can do to help?

There was a short pause before Sam's next text appeared.

> I know you're busy, but Maddie does have one request I think you can help with. She'd really love to have some flowers by her bed

> I'll head into town and pick some up. Shouldn't take long.

> Thanks Chris.

"Hey Norman," Chris called out. "I have to make a quick run into Waterford. Keep setting things up until I get back."

"Will do." Norman squinted at Chris, noticing his concern. "Everything okay?"

Chris hesitated, his gaze drifting towards the farmhouse where the young girl lay battling her illness. "I'm not sure, Norm," he admitted quietly. "Maddie's not doing well. I'm going to make a run to get her some flowers."

"Flowers, huh?" Norman repeated, his voice softening. "That's nice of you, man... hope she feels better soon."

"Me too," Chris echoed, before climbing into his truck and driving away.

The drive to Waterford was a blur. The town was bustling with life, people going about their routines unaware of events happening around them. Chris stopped at a local florist, picking out a bouquet of flowers that seemed to hold the essence of innocence and hope. Delicate baby's breath intertwined with lacy Queen Anne's lace, while white daisies and yellow buttercups added a splash of color. They were simple yet held a beauty that felt fitting for Maddie.

Feeling a sense of urgency, Chris cradled the bouquet carefully as he headed back. The lush green fields and gently rolling hills seemed to take on a solemn beauty; a reminder that even in the darkest moments, there was still hope to be found.

I stood at the top of the stairs, watching as Chris carefully climbed each step, cradling the bouquet of flowers in his arms. I held a finger to my lips, gesturing for Chris to be quiet.

"Hey," Chris said softly as he reached the landing. "How's she doing?"

"Resting," I replied, my voice catching as I glanced back into the room. "Kats with her."

"I got these for her." Chris shifted his grip on the flowers and held them out to me.

"That's sweet of you... Maddie will love them." I gestured for him to follow me downstairs to the kitchen. I pulled open a cupboard and retrieved a vase, filling it with water as Chris laid the bouquet on the counter.

"She had a really bad episode this afternoon... she was choking and couldn't breathe."

"Has that happened before?"

"Never this bad," I admitted, my hands shaking slightly as I arranged the flowers in the vase. "We've been using her nebulizer since the attack." A moment of silence passed before Chris broke the quiet.

"Sam, how is she really doing?"

I glanced at him and smiled, knowing he wanted nothing more than to help in any way that he could. I hesitated, swallowing the lump in my throat before answering.

"I can't shake this feeling that she's slipping away from me."

Chris's grip on my shoulder tightened, offering silent support as we stood in the dimly lit kitchen.

"I wanted to take Maddie to the hospital today, but she said no." My eyes filled with tears as I recounted the conversation. "She begged me not to make her go, to let her stay here with you, Kat, and Norman. She said she'd never leave Amelia."

Chris's brow furrowed. "Do you think the hospital would be better for her?" he asked gently.

"I'm not sure," I confessed, feeling a weight on my chest. "Given the kind of sickness she has, it's just hard to say. I do know Maddie couldn't stand being in the hospital during previous treatments. She was always scared she wouldn't make it back home."

"Sam, do you think Maddie is close to dying?"

I hesitated, unable to find the words. The thought of losing her threatened to shatter me into a million pieces. "I don't know," I finally managed, my voice trembling. "But if she doesn't show some strength soon..." My words trailed off as tears filled my eyes. "I can't believe I'm talking so calmly about my baby dying," I choked out, my hands shaking as I gripped the edge of the counter.

"Hey," Chris whispered, pulling me into a comforting embrace. "We're here... we're not going anywhere. We'll do everything we can for both of you."

Taking a deep breath, I tried to steady myself, pulling away from his caress. "How's the dig going?" I asked, desperate to shift my focus onto something else.

"We'll start soon," he replied, his voice strong and reassuring. "I'm planning to dig through the night.

Hopefully we'll find Amelia's remains quickly and put her to rest. I think Maddie will gain some strength from that."

"God, I hope you're right," I whispered, looking heavenward as if searching for answers. "I pray that's true."

Chris turned to head outside, and I slowly climbed the stairs to Maddie's room. The delicate petals of the flowers swayed gently, releasing their sweet scent into the room. Maddie's eyes fluttered open, and a weak smile graced her lips when she saw the flowers. Kat was sitting beside her, gently stroking her hair.

"Chris got these for you."

"They're beautiful," Maddie whispered, her voice filled with warmth. I placed the vase on the table by Maddie's bed, the vibrant colors of the flowers providing a stark contrast against the crisp white sheets. Maddie's eyes followed my every move, a mixture of curiosity and wonder dancing within them.

"Mama?" she questioned, her voice fragile like autumn leaves in a breeze. I sat gently on the edge of the bed, my heart aching to see her so weak. A tender smile played on my lips as I reached for her frail hand.

"What is it, Maddie?"

"Can we... can we leave the flowers here?" she asked, her eyes never leaving the bouquet. "I want to see them when I wake up."

"Of course, sweetheart," I assured her, giving her hand a gentle squeeze.

"Mama, am I going to die?"

Maddie's question pierced the silence like a knife. The weight of those words was almost too much to bear, and my heart tightened as if squeezed in a vice.

"Yes, sweetheart," I choked out, trying to keep my voice from breaking. "One day you will, but you won't be alone. I'll be right here with you." Her wide eyes searched my face for reassurance, and I couldn't help but marvel at her innocence.

"Will it hurt?" she asked, her tiny voice trembling.

I took a deep breath, gathering what little strength I had left. "No, darling. It won't hurt. You'll feel like you're going to sleep. No more pain. No more struggles. Just sleep."

Maddie nodded, the words settling into her young mind like gentle snowflakes on the ground. Her gaze shifted to the window, where the setting sun cast a golden glow across the room.

"I don't want to leave you," she whispered, tears trickling down her pale cheeks.

My own tears fell like raindrops as I leaned down to kiss her forehead. "I know, baby. And I don't want you to go. But it's not up to us, and sometimes, we just have to say goodbye."

Maddie sighed, caught between acceptance and melancholy. "Will you be sad?"

I smiled through my tears, stroking her hand. "I will be, sweetheart. I will miss you every day. But I'll also be grateful for the time we've had together, and I'll carry your love with me always."

Fatigue began to claim her, and Maddie's eyes fluttered. "I love you, Mama."

"I love you more than all the stars in the sky," I whispered, holding her hand against my heart, as the last light of day faded from the room.

⇢⇢ ·•· ⇠⇠

Chris surveyed the area around the well. He paced back and forth, mentally preparing himself for the task ahead. Norman walked to the main power box and flipped a switch. Instantly, lights illuminated the well site, bathing everything in a bright glow.

"Everything's ready," Norman called out, walking over to join him. "Should I start the cameras rolling?"

Chris nodded, his eyes betraying a sense of urgency. "Yeah, let's get this started."

Norman headed to the van and reappeared moments later, signaling with a thumbs up. Muttering a short prayer under his breath, Chris gripped the pickaxe tightly and began to break ground near the center of the well. Each swing felt like an act of resolve, slicing through layers of earth and history. After a few repetitions he paused to catch his breath. Norman joined him, filling buckets with the loose rock and dirt. Chris glanced around, noticing fireflies had begun to appear. Their delicate dance seemed almost curious, as if they were watching the events unfold.

"Bugs are back," Chris murmured, his gaze tracking the insect's movements.

Norman nodded, a hint of a smile playing on his lips. "Figures... they seem to make an appearance when big things like this go down. Think they can sense what's going on with Maddie?"

"Maybe. I'd like to believe that," Chris sighed.

"Think she'll make it?" Norman asked abruptly.

"Hard to say," Chris replied, his voice tinged with sadness. "Sam knew this day would come eventually, but I don't think she's ready for it to be now. I don't think any of us are."

"Do you think Amelia is making it happen quicker?" Norman asked, "I mean, it's taken its toll on Maddie, having Amelia around... we've all seen that."

"Maybe." Chris looked at the foot deep hole he'd made in the ground, a little frustrated with the slow progress. "If she is, we need to get this hole dug. The sooner we put Maddie's spirit to rest, the sooner things will get better."

Fireflies sparkled in the twilight, their wings fluttering in choreographed patterns. Chris drove the pickaxe into the ground with determination. It rose and fell in a regular rhythm, its tip glinting in the bright lights. The reverberations echoed across the field with each strike, forming a constant beat against the backdrop of a gentle breeze blowing through tall grass.

Thump.

Thump.

Thump.

※

Kat was slouched in a corner of the room, her face buried in her hands. I couldn't tell if she was sleeping or just deep in thought. Outside I could hear the constant pounding, a rhythmic cadence that mimicked the beat of my heart. Maddie's room was quiet, the soft hum of the nebulizer a steady background to her shallow breaths.

"Mama," she whispered, her voice like the brush of butterfly's wings against my soul. "I talked to Amelia today."

"Amelia?" I couldn't help but frown. "What did she say to you?"

Maddie's eyes drifted to the corner of her bedroom, where a soft, green light began to dance. "Amelia told me they would be with me tonight... and there they are." She pointed towards the window, where fireflies had begun to gather; one, two, then six or more. The air seemed to shimmer, alive with the presence of something beyond understanding. I gasped, captivated by the mystical display.

Maddie shifted in her bed, as if finding comfort in sharing the secrets of another realm. "Amelia said dying is like becoming a firefly. You don't really leave, you just become part of the light. Love is the light, Mama. It never goes away."

Kat dropped her hands and looked straight at Maddie. Makeup smeared her face as tears coursed down her cheeks. Maddie's words had touched her in a way that I could only imagine. She stood and gave a brief nod before making her way towards the stairs. "I need some air," she declared as she vanished into the shadows below.

"Look," Maddie whispered, her hand trembling as she pointed out the window towards the sky. "The stars are coming out."

I stood and moved to the window, my eyes lingering on

the tiny specs of light just beginning to form. Outside, the world seemed to hold its breath, waiting for night to fall. "Beautiful, aren't they?" I said, smiling through my tears.

"Love is light, Mama," Maddie whispered. "Just like the stars."

Her words resonated deep within my soul, providing a sense of comfort, and understanding that I hadn't known was possible. "Sweetheart," I said softly, my voice thick with emotion, "do you really believe that?"

She nodded without hesitation, her conviction unwavering.

"Then I'll believe it too."

Kat sprinted through the darkened house. Bursting through the back door, she collapsed onto the porch steps. The cold evening air bit at her face as the tears flowed freely, mixing with streaks of mascara that ran down her cheeks like ink on a rain-soaked page.

"Hey, Chris," Norman called out, "Kats on the back porch... she looks upset."

Chris paused mid swing and turned to look. A wave of fear washed over him as he dropped the pickaxe. "Stay here, Norman. I'll go see what's going on."

"I can talk to her if you want," Norman offered, but Chris shook his head.

"No, it's better if I check on things," he replied as he began striding across the field. "You keep digging."

Chris hesitated for a moment before sitting down next to Kat. The sound of her crying tugged at his heart, making it difficult to find the right thing to say.

"Kat," he began gently, "is everything okay with Maddie?"

Through her tears, she managed to speak. "Yeah, she's resting. Sam's with her."

"Thank God... I was afraid..." his words caught in his throat, and he decided not to express what they all feared. "This is tough, isn't it... we all feel it."

Kat tried to regain her composure, brushing her bangs from her face with one hand as she motioned for Chris to stop speaking. "It's just me... just another crazy day at the office," she choked out, trying to brush him off.

Chris wasn't deterred. "Talk to me, Kat," he insisted.

Taking a deep breath, she relented. "It's not just Maddie... there's more to it. She's talking to Sam... saying things... talking about dying. It's just... it got to me, you know?"

"Maddie's talking about dying?" Chris asked, surprised. "What did she say?"

"Oh wow... where do I begin." Kat wiped her cheeks and sighed heavily. "She says Amelia told her things today... stuff about how everything's connected, and how when we die, we become light."

Chris nodded thoughtfully, his eyes searching Kat's face. "Do you think Maddie can sense it's coming?"

"I think things are a little more real... and I think Amelia is steering her to think that way," Kat whispered, wiping her eyes. "But I hope the things coming outta that kid's mouth are true."

"What kind of things?" Chris questioned, trying to understand her thoughts.

"Basically, that we're eternal... and we join others as light after we die," she replied, her voice barely a whisper. "I've always wondered if there was something more out there, something we can't see or touch. But hearing Maddie talk about it, it just... it made me feel like maybe there's hope, you know?"

"Hope for what?" Chris asked tenderly, sensing there was more to her words.

"For finding answers, for understanding the unknown, and maybe even for reconnecting with those we've lost." The two sat in silence for a while, their thoughts mingling with the night air. "Chris," Kat began hesitantly. "My mom died when I was just a kid. I've spent my whole life trying to make sense of it, why she had to go, why I had to grow up without her." She fiddled with the hem of her jacket, avoiding his gaze. "For years, I felt so bitter, so alone. All I wanted was a chance to be close to her again, in some way."

"Is that why you joined our team?"

"Yeah," Kat admitted with a slight chuckle. "It's why I became so obsessed with spooks. I thought maybe, just maybe, I could find a way to reach her." She looked at him, her dark eyes glistening. "I've never told that to anyone... and please don't tell Normie. He'll find some way to twist it into something weird to torture me."

"It'll stay between us, I promise," Chris murmured, placing a supportive hand on her shoulder.

"Thanks," she whispered, wiping away a tear that

escaped down her cheek. "This whole thing with Amelia... I mean, I've seen her. I know now that there *is* something out there... life beyond, you know?"

"Amelia's really shaken things up for me too," Chris admitted. "I mean, I've never come across anything as mind-blowingly real as what we've gone through with her. It's cranked up my belief big time."

"Wait... you're Mr. Paranormal Investigator... the expert. Are you saying you never believed in any of this before now?"

"I've believed... I've just not experienced it like this before. If anything, I've always thought the spiritual world was the real world, and this physical world was just an expression of it. Your mom is out there, waiting for you... you'll find her."

A wave of gratitude washed over Kat as she hugged Chris tightly. "Thanks boss," she whispered into his ear. "You're one of the good ones. I don't care what Norman says about you."

"Wait, what?" Chris questioned, returning her embrace.

Kat responded with a playful grin, her gaze casually glancing away as if to convey that she was done with the conversation.

Chapter Sixteen

Let Your Demons Devour You

June, 1961

Laine paced the length of his veranda behind the mansion, his shoes tapping against the stone floor as the damp air clung to his skin. It was a hot night, humid and oppressive. It was difficult to breathe. Sweat trickled down his face, a cooling sensation that did little to quell the fire that raged within him. The darkness of the night was nearly absolute, with only the dim glow of a few lanterns from the nearby stable breaking through the void.

In his hand, Laine carried a half-empty tumbler of whiskey. He had finished one bottle in his office earlier that night, an inadequate attempt to numb his frayed nerves. Fetching the tumbler from the bar in the great room had led to a series of stumbles, his anger mingling with the liquor to make him unsteady on his feet. Furniture had met his wrath, each collision fueling his growing fury. His rage was real, fueled by fear and despair.

"Goddammit," Laine muttered under his breath, his voice barely audible above the distant sounds of insects chirring in the night. Allison's threat hung over him like a guillotine, the blade poised to sever everything he held dear. She planned to expose him, and the knowledge left him feeling powerless, trapped. Laine's mind raced, desperate for a solution, but the alcohol clouding his thoughts offered no reprieve.

"No... no you can't." he groaned, his words slurred as he took another swig of whiskey, the burn doing nothing to dull the sharp edge of his despair.

His thoughts turned dark, images of violence and retribution flickering through his mind like a twisted reel of film. He imagined himself confronting Allison, his hands clenched into fists as he demanded her silence. The thought was both sickening and tantalizing, a forbidden fantasy that only served to highlight the depths of his desperation.

"Allison...you can't...can't let you," Laine slurred to himself as the vision played out. His thoughts swirled in a chaotic whirlwind, each one darker and more twisted than the last. He could feel his sanity teetering on the edge of a precipice, and he was powerless to stop it. The whiskey burned his throat as he took another gulp. His demons were relentless, clawing at his mind, pushing him further into madness.

The hot, sticky night pressed down on him, suffocating both his body and soul. He could feel the darkness swallowing him whole. Gasping for air, Laine stumbled to the edge of the porch and fell to his knees, the impact sending sharp, painful jolts through his legs. A loud thud echoed through the night, followed by another, and another. Each one reverberated in Laine's mind like the tolling of a bell, grating on his already frayed nerves. It took a moment for him to realize the noise was coming from the nearby stable, where a horse had begun kicking its stall door in agitation.

"Will you shut that damn beast up!" Laine screamed, his voice hoarse and ragged as he called for the stable groom. But the relentless pounding persisted, each thud slicing through the air like a knife, taunting him with its unyielding rhythm.

"Make it... make it stop!" he roared, his voice cracking under the strain. But there was no answer, no reprieve from the sound that seemed determined to drive him over the edge.

Laine's thoughts spiraled, untethered from reality. As the horse's hooves continued to pound against the stable door, the sound morphed in his mind, becoming something far more sinister. He imagined each thunderous blow was the impact of his own fists pummeling Allison, every hit bringing him closer to freedom from her and the secret they shared.

"Damn you!" he roared, hurling the tumbler at the ground. It shattered on impact, amber liquid seeping into the thirsty earth. Trembling, Laine reached for the broken glass, aching for one more sip of the numbing whiskey. His fingers closed around a jagged shard, and it sliced deeply into his palm. Laine howled, more from the torment within than the pain of his injury.

He stood unsteadily to his feet, his hand bleeding profusely. The relentless thuds echoed in his ears. To Laine, each pounding blow was an extension of his own rage, his desire for control. Clutching his wounded hand, he wandered through the great room towards the front door, leaving a trail of crimson that marred the intricate patterns of the Persian rugs. Evil had overtaken him, twisting his once rational mind into a black vortex of desperation and violence. "I swear... I'll end this..." he mumbled, as he opened the heavy wooden door and stumbled outside.

He staggered towards the Rolls-Royce Silver Cloud parked near the end of the driveway, its sleek form a monstrous silhouette. The driver, half asleep in the front seat, jolted awake at the sound of approaching footsteps. He snapped to attention, leaping from his seat to open the back door for Laine.

"Evening, Mr. Laine," he said, trying to mask his alarm at Laine's disheveled appearance. "Where would you like to go, sir?"

"Out... my way!" Laine snarled, shoving the driver aside as he slammed the rear door shut.

"Sir, please, you're in no condition to –" the driver began to protest, only to be silenced by Laine's rage.

"Get away!" Laine bellowed, his voice cracking with fury. He shoved the driver to the ground, feeling a twisted satisfaction as the man gasped in pain. Laine climbed into the driver's seat and started the limo with trembling hands. The engine roared to life and Laine stomped on the accelerator. The car swerved and careened down the driveway, leaving the bewildered driver sprawled on the pavement.

Upstairs in her bedroom, Julia stood by the window,

her breath fogging the glass as she peered down onto the driveway below. She had never seen Lawrence like this before, but she couldn't say it surprised her. Lawrence was nothing more than a caged animal, trapped with no way out.

She watched as the car sped away, the taillights casting eerie red shadows on the trees lining the road. Julia knew this was the beginning of the end. There was no sadness in her heart for the man she had once loved, only a cold bitterness now filled that space. She closed the curtains and retreated to the sanctuary of her bed, the crisp sheets offering little comfort.

"Let your demons devour you," she thought bitterly, staring at the ceiling as if challenging some unseen force. "You brought this on yourself."

The barn loft was lit by the pale glow of a battery-operated lantern, casting long shadows on the piles of old hay that formed makeshift walls. The space was cramped, with barely enough room to stand, yet it had served as Amelia's haven for years. A soft mattress lay on the worn wooden floor, covered with a sleeping bag that had seen better days. Several dolls were scattered about, their button eyes staring into the darkness, keeping watch over Amelia and her mother, Allison.

Outside the barn, the night was warm and humid. Allison opened the small window at the edge of the loft, where a pulley and rope hung, remnants of a time when it was used to lower hay to the ground below.

"Look, Mama," Amelia said, holding up the ribbon Angel Laine had given her. Her eyes sparkled with excitement as she continued, "Someday, I'm gonna have my very own horse and win ribbons at horse shows, just like Angel does." Her fingers traced the delicate edges of the ribbon, feeling its silky smoothness. Allison smiled softly as she laid down beside her, brushing a stray lock of hair from Amelia's glistening forehead. "I believe that too, and I'll be right beside you, cheering you on." Allison smiled tenderly at her daughter, their bodies close together on the soft bed.

"Why are we sleeping in the hideaway tonight instead of in the house?" Amelia's curiosity was evident in her wide eyes. "It's so hot in here."

Allison hesitated, choosing her words carefully. "Well, in a way, it has to do with Angel, and the show at her place... the one she invited you to. It seems some people don't want us to be there, and they said some things that worried me."

"Promise me we're going!" Amelia pleaded, her voice filled with determination.

"Don't worry," Allison agreed, thinking of the truths she planned to reveal. "We'll be there, but for now it's better we play it safe and sleep out here."

"But why... why wouldn't they want us to go?"

"Because..." Allison hesitated, her voice filled with emotion, "...because it would reveal a secret."

"What secret?" Amelia's eyes widened with interest.

Allison took a deep breath, feeling the weight of the

moment. She reached into the pocket of her dress and pulled out a small velvet box. "I've got a little something for you. This was given to me shortly after you were born, and I've been saving it for you, waiting for the right time." Her voice trembled as she spoke, her love for Amelia evident in every word. "I believe now is that time."

With a soft click, Allison opened the velvet box, revealing a beautiful golden locket. It was adorned with intricate engravings of flowers and vines, perfect for a young girl. A tiny keyhole begged to be opened, hinting at a hidden treasure within.

"Wow," Amelia whispered in amazement.

"This locket," Allison continued, her voice filled with emotion, "was a gift from your father. But he didn't even know what it was. He... wasn't happy that you were born."

"Why not, Mama?"

Allison paused, her heart heavy with truth. She looked over at the worn storybook they'd flipped through a thousand times, its spine creased from years of reading. Taking a deep breath, she continued.

"Amelia," she said softly, "remember the witch in the story book we've read? How people talked about her being evil and ugly, but she really wasn't?"

Amelia nodded as she recalled the tale of the misunderstood enchantress.

"Those people didn't know her," Allison explained. "They were afraid of her because they believed she could hurt them or ruin their lives. Your father felt that way about you."

"But he didn't know anything about me."

Allison smiled sadly, acknowledging her daughter's innocence. "You're right. It wasn't about you. It was about him. I agreed not to tell anyone who your father was to keep you safe. You were a secret."

Amelia furrowed her brow, still struggling to understand.

Allison pulled the locket from the velvet box and held it closer for her to see. "Your father didn't know how special this locket would be one day. I want you to have it now, with all my love. When you wear it, remember... I'll always be with you."

Allison reached to place the locket around Amelia's neck.

"Who is my father, Mama?"

Allison's hands froze and her fingers trembled as she clutched the delicate chain. Her eyes filled with tears as she looked into Amelia's expectant gaze. "Honey, your father is --" The words caught in her throat, a lump forming as she tried to force them out."

The sudden roar of a car engine shattered the silence, tearing through the night like a wild beast. Tires screeched and gravel flew as the vehicle charged through the front gate and onto the property, coming to an abrupt halt near the farmhouse. Allison's heart pounded in her chest, fear gripping her tightly as she hurriedly returned the locket to her pocket and extinguished the lantern. In the darkness, she whispered urgently to Amelia, "Stay put and don't make a sound, no matter what. I'll come for you when it's safe."

Amelia nodded, fear worming its way into her chest as the pounding on the door outside echoed through the barn like gunshots. The dark hideaway that had once felt cozy and secure now seemed suffocating and treacherous.

Allison made her way to the ladder, the air in the loft heavy with tension and dread. Climbing down into the barn below, she stumbled over a few of Amelia's toys, her pulse racing as she reached the door. Peeking outside, she saw a dark figure, pacing and screaming her name.

"Allison... Allison we need to talk. Open the door... I know you're here."

Panic surged through her body; she knew she had to act fast. Allison darted through the darkness and jumped up the back porch stairs and into the kitchen. Adrenaline coursed through her body as she rushed through the darkened entry way and into the front room. With the flick of a switch, a blinding light illuminated the area. She shielded her eyes before opening the door, her breath seizing in a startled gasp as she found herself face-to-face with Lawrence Laine.

Allison's heart raced as she took in Lawrence's disheveled state, his unkempt hair, wild eyes and sweat-streaked face. The air around him was heavy with the scent of alcohol and desperation.

"Lawrence," she said coolly, trying to hide the tremor in her voice. "What are you doing here?"

For a moment, Lawrence's rage seemed to recede as he looked at Allison. She was just as beautiful as he remembered, stirring memories of their secret love affair and the passionate embraces they once shared. But the fleeting tenderness he felt was quickly swallowed by the darkness that had overtaken his soul.

"You know why I'm here," he snarled, his voice thick and slurred. "You've gone against me... your promise."

Allison could see the battle being waged in Laine's mind, the struggle between his lingering feelings for her and the fury that consumed him. She backed away from him as he staggered through the door.

"Lawrence, I haven't gone back on my word, you have. Where have you been for the past nine years? What about the promises you made to me?"

Laine staggered and fell against the door frame, his mind a storm of conflicting thoughts. The ghost of their past swirled around him like a vengeful specter, threatening to drag him under. Images flashed through his mind, tender moments, stolen kisses, passionate nights, only to be replaced with visions of his own destruction, all brought about by the very woman who once held his heart.

"Nobody will know of this... of us." Laine hissed, the slurring of his words punctuated by a piercing stare.

"They'll know about Amelia," Allison shot back coldly. "It's time everyone knows the truth."

Laine flinched at the mention of the name, as if struck by an unseen force. "Amelia," he spat, the name dripping with venom. Allison cautiously stepped back as she allowed her words to sink in.

"This isn't about us, is it...it's about her. You really think you can use that child to ruin me?"

"Lawrence, please," Allison pleaded, her eyes filling with tears. "We're not trying to hurt you. We just want our lives to be better."

Your lives?" Laine snarled, his fury prevailing at last. His fists tightened, and the muscles of his face contorted into a menacing expression. Lawrence Laine was a man teetering on the brink of insanity.

"Where is she, Allison?" he demanded, slurring his words slightly as he stared her down. His gaze was a storm of conflicting emotions: fury, fear, and something that almost resembled guilt. "Where are you hiding her?"

"Lawrence, please," Allison implored, stumbling as she backed away. "She's not here. You're scaring me."

"Scaring you?" Laine screamed. "You have no idea what fear is... what it's like to have your whole world threatened by one little secret." He looked at her with wild, accusing eyes. "This ends tonight, Allison. I won't live in fear any longer."

In one swift movement, Laine lunged at Allison, throwing her to the floor as he called out Amelia's name in a frenzy. The house reverberated with loud bangs as he tossed aside furniture, frantically moving through each room in search of the little girl.

Allison gasped for breath, pain radiating through her body from the impact. She knew she had to get Laine away from the barn where Amelia was hiding. Gathering every ounce of strength she had left, she screamed at him, "*She isn't here!*"

Laine's eyes narrowed as he staggered back into the room, his face contorted. "You're lying," he snarled. "I will find her." He lunged at Allison again, but she managed to dodge his grasp, bolting for the door.

Her scream pierced the night air as she ran outside and into the field, the tall grass whipping against her legs. The sound of Laine's heavy footsteps followed closely behind, his own voice a guttural roar demanding that she stop. Desperation clawed at her thoughts, urging her to keep moving forward, to lead Laine away from her precious daughter.

※ ⋅⋅◆⋅⋅ ※

Amelia's heart raced, pounding in her ears like a drumbeat as she listened to the commotion coming from the farmhouse. The desperate screams and shouts of her name filled her with terror. She couldn't understand who this monster was that attacked her mother or why he called her name with such hatred.

She pressed her face against the warm glass of the loft window, pushing it open just enough to get a better view of the unfolding nightmare. Her eyes widened in horror as she saw her mother fleeing into the field with a large, menacing figure close behind. Amelia knew she had to do something; she couldn't let this animal take her mother away from her.

Ignoring her mother's plea to stay hidden in the loft, Amelia made up her mind. With trembling hands, she climbed down the ladder, the rough wood scraping against her skin. As soon as her feet hit the ground, she sprinted out of the open barn door and into the dark field.

Time seemed to slow as the horror before her grew closer. The world around her blurred at the edges, giving way to a nightmarish landscape of shadows and monsters.

Amelia's heart pounded in her ears, drowning out her mother's screams as she crouched low to the ground. "I have to help her," she thought, her mind reeling as she watched.

- - -

Allison's breaths came in ragged gasps as she stumbled across the uneven ground. Laine's footsteps echoed behind her, growing louder with every second.

"Stop!" he screamed, his hoarse voice a piercing cry. "Stop!" he roared again, each repetition more twisted and furious than the last.

Allison felt herself begin to falter as her foot caught on something hidden. She stumbled and fell forward, the world spinning around in dizzying circles. She crashed to the ground, her vision blurred from the hard fall. Laine's fingers dug into her dress, wrenching her onto her back to face him. He stood over her like a vengeful specter, his bloodied hand still seeping crimson.

"Please," she whispered, her plea lost in the wind.

"Where is she?" Laine demanded once more, his voice a guttural snarl.

Panic clawed at Allison's throat as she half-crawled, half-dragged herself away. She scrambled to her feet, but Laine's bloody hand shot out, gripping her arm with bruising force. He shook her, his face contorted with fury, and screamed the question that had become his mantra: "WHERE IS SHE?"

"Sh-she's not here!" Allison choked out, tears streaming down her face. Laine's grip tightened.

"LIAR!" he bellowed, striking her face with his bloody

hand. The force of the blow sent her sprawling, ears ringing as stars danced before her eyes. As she teetered on the edge of consciousness, a shrill sound pierced the darkness... Amelia's scream.

"Leave her alone!"

For a moment, everything seemed to stop, suspended in time as the echoes of Amelia's cry hung in the air. Laine spun toward the sound, his wild eyes searching the darkness. There, in the shadows of the tall grass, he spotted the small, crouched form.

"Amelia?" His voice was a mixture of disbelief and desperation. Silence hung heavy in the air, punctuated only by their ragged breaths. He took a step toward her, his voice softening. "Amelia... come here."

A shiver ran down Amelia's spine. This man knew her name, and he wanted her for some reason she couldn't imagine.

"Stay away from me!" she cried, her voice trembling. She turned and sprinted toward the farmhouse, her legs pumping furiously, her mind filled with images of her mother's battered face and haunted eyes. Laine gave chase, calling her name over and over, the sound becoming a haunting echo in the night. He had to see this child, his child, with his own eyes.

The wind whispered through the tall grass, its warm tendrils wrapping around Amelia as she raced towards the farmhouse. The monstrous figure behind her roared her name, his bloodied clothes clinging to his sweat-slicked skin. To Amelia, he sounded like a wolf in the night, growling and gnashing its teeth as it pursued its prey.

"Please," she thought, her heart pounding, "please let me make it."

Her breaths came in sharp, stinging gasps, each inhale a desperate attempt to fill her burning lungs. Fear clouded her mind, making her steps feel heavy and clumsy. She could hear the creature's snarls growing louder behind her, a relentless predator snapping at her heels. Fear and adrenaline coursed through her veins, propelling her forward on unsteady legs. The farmhouse loomed ahead, its dark silhouette a sanctuary in the moonless night. The thick grass snagged at her feet, while stones hidden beneath it threatened to trip her with every step.

"Mama, please," she thought desperately, praying for some kind of guidance. The world around Amelia seemed to warp and shift. The once-familiar landscape contorted into a twisted, nightmarish version of itself. Trees reached out like gnarled claws, while the very ground beneath her feet appeared to roil and undulate until it disappeared completely.

With one last, frantic lunge, Laine reached for her, his fingers barely brushing against her small form before she vanished into the dark. He hurtled forward, falling and crashing through a poorly constructed stone wall. The impact sent the stones scattering across the ground, a few grazing his face and drawing blood. His shoulder burned with a searing pain, and he couldn't stifle the scream that tore from his lips.

"Godammit!" he screamed in agony, confusion lacing his voice. He forced himself to his knees as he tried to focus on his surroundings. The alcohol coursing through his veins made everything feel surreal, as if he were trapped in some twisted dream. He expected to see the young girl lying unconscious in front of him, but what greeted him instead was an abyssal void.

"Where are you?"

His eyes adjusted to the shadows. There was something there, something darker than the surrounding grass; a hole in the ground, about four feet wide and impossibly dark. In that moment, the meaning behind the stones clicked in his mind, chilling him to the bone. He was staring at a well.

He crawled forward and knelt next to the gaping pit, pushing some broken boards away from the opening. He was sure others had fallen into the abyss, alongside the child. He stared into the black void, his stomach churning with dread.

A gut-wrenching cry pierced the night. Allison, her face streaked with tears, managed to get to her feet. Her body trembled as she began walking towards the dark figure kneeling in the field. Each step grew more determined as she regained her strength, fear driving her forward.

"Lawrence!" she screamed, her voice raw and desperate. Laine remained hunched over, motionless, his gaze locked onto the gaping maw of the well.

Allison gasped as she hobbled over and stood beside Laine. The fear of this man, who had struck her down moments before, now paled in comparison to the terror that gripped her soul. The well, its darkness seemingly infinite, taunted her with its sinister darkness.

"Amelia!" she screamed, her voice shaking with the weight of despair. "Baby, please, no!"

Kneeling at the edge of the dark opening, Allison's tears fell like raindrops into the abyss below, her body wracked with sobs for the daughter she knew had fallen inside.

Laine, still reeling from the collision with the stone wall, struggled to his feet. He reached out, placing a trembling hand on Allison's heaving shoulder.

"*Get away from me!*" Allison shrieked, shrinking from Laine's touch. She couldn't bear to have him near her, not after what he'd done.

He knew that any attempt at consolation would be futile, but the gesture was all he could offer amidst the chaos of his thoughts. Within him, a battle raged; demons clawed at the edges of his mind, their whispers unrelenting. His fear replaced any doubt that lingered, and as the voices grew louder, Laine felt himself surrender to their desires. His grip on Allison's shoulder tightened, his fingertips digging into her flesh.

"Forgive me," he rasped, as though releasing a final, desperate plea for salvation.

Allison's scream tore through the night like a banshee's wail before dissolving into an eerie silence that seemed to swallow the entire field.

Laine's voice choked with emotion as he stared at the well. His vision swam with shadows, phantoms born of alcohol and rage. He had fallen into madness, unable to distinguish truth from illusion.

"I'm sorry," he whispered into the void, his voice raw and broken. There was no reply... only silence.

Chapter Seventeen

"Bucket's Full"

Sam's eyelids fluttered, her mind drifting in a dreamlike state. Everything around her blurred and fused together. Bright colors blended into odd hues before dissipating into a cold black and white. Sam found herself sitting in front of the TV, the ghostly images flickering on the screen as she watched an old re-run of Lawrence Laine's Starlight Review. The scene played out before her as if it were real, every detail vivid and lifelike. Laine stood center stage, his ageless charisma commanding the audience's attention. Despite his mid-forties' appearance, there was something timeless about him.

Sam stared at the screen. She felt disconnected from her own body as though she were merely a passive observer, watching a memory that wasn't her own. Her fingers reached out to switch off the TV but paused just as they brushed against the knob. Music filled the room, drawing her focus back to the screen. A young woman stepped forward and began to sing.

In shadows deep, I took my flight,

K. D. PHILLIPS

> *Lost in the veil of endless night.*
> *A child once, with dreams so bright,*
> *Now a whisper, a ghostly sight.*

    Sam stood, her body tense and trembling. The weight of the past few days bore down on her like an oppressive fog. Amelia's desperate cries for help haunted her, while nightmarish creatures stalked her under the cover of darkness. And now, Maddie's illness had returned with a vengeance, threatening to snatch away the light in her life.
    The singer's eyes seemed to bore into her, as if she could see the depths of her despair. For a moment, Sam felt as though she were no longer alone in her struggles, that there was someone, somewhere, who understood her pain, and shared her burden. The room stretched and warped around her, the walls receding into darkness until they were swallowed by an inky void. The flickering images on the television screen bled out into reality, and the singer stepped forward, her once ethereal form solidifying into a tangible presence.
    "Help me," Sam whispered, her voice trembling as the spectral woman drew near. The air grew cold and heavy, thick with the weight of unspeakable sorrow. The singer looked at Sam with an intensity that seemed to pierce her very soul, her eyes mirrors reflecting the pain that had consumed them both. Her voice once again filled the darkness surrounding them.

> *A mother's love, a daughter's grace,*

FIREFLIES

The answers lie in time and space.
Healing waits in truth's embrace,
For in understanding, we find our place.

The lyrics swirled around them like tendrils of smoke. Sam felt herself being pulled deeper into the darkness. The room around her dissolved into an endless expanse of shadow, leaving her clinging to the lyrics and as if they were a lifeline.

Healing waits in truth's embrace...

The haunting words continued to echo in Sam's mind, growing louder with each repetition. "*Please*," she cried out, desperately wanting to understand.

I jolted awake, my heart racing, my body drenched in sweat. I blinked, trying to shake off the remnants of my dream. The mid-afternoon light cast a dim, eerie glow in Maddie's room. I looked at her lying next to me. She seemed so fragile, as if she might slip away at any moment.

"Please don't be afraid," I whispered, reaching out to touch her clammy hand. "I'm right here... right here with you."

Maddie's sunken eyes remained closed, her once rosy cheeks now as pale as the sheets she lay on. Beads of sweat dotted her brow, and her breaths came shallow and labored. I longed to see her bright smile and hear her laughter again, but those memories felt like they belonged to another lifetime.

As I sat by her side, watching her struggle for each breath, a heaviness settled in my chest. My thoughts mingled with those of my recent nightmare. "Was it all just a dream?" I wondered, trying to make sense of the harrowing vision. "I remember that song... that singer. I've heard it before." The more I tried to cling to the details of the dream, the more they slipped through my fingers like sand. "Healing waits in truth's embrace?" I muttered to myself, racking my brain for any hidden meaning to the haunting lyrics.

"Mama, I'm cold," Maddie whispered, stirring me from my thoughts. I tucked the blanket closer to her sides and rubbed her arms.

The rare moments Maddie spoke sent chills through me. The deep, raspy tone of her voice belonged to Amelia, not the Maddie I knew and loved. Her words were few, but they echoed in my mind: pleas for help, urgent whispers to hurry, and heart-wrenching cries of pain. My stomach twisted into knots at the thought that this might be Maddie's last day on earth.

"Not today," I whispered, squeezing Maddie's hand. "Hang on, baby."

I heard footsteps coming up the stairs and turned to see Kat enter the room, carrying a tray with snacks and glasses of water. Her dark eyes scanned the scene, taking in Maddie's fragile form and my own haggard appearance. She tried to smile, but I could see the worry etched on her face.

"Howdy," she said softly, trying to keep the atmosphere light despite the gravity of the situation. "I brought you something to munch on... gotta keep your strength up."

"Thanks, Kat," I replied, my voice hoarse from lack of sleep. "That's sweet of you."

"Want me to open a bag of chips for you," she asked, setting the tray down on the bedside table. "Salt and vinegar... you're fav."

The thought of food made my stomach churn, and I shook my head. "Maybe later, but right now... I just... can't."

Kat sighed, understanding my struggle, and sat down beside me on the edge of the bed. "How you holdin' up?" she asked, her voice gentle.

"Truthfully? I'm terrified," I admitted, my eyes returning to Maddie's pale face. "I can't lose her."

"We're all scared," Kat said, placing a comforting hand on my shoulder. "I believe she'll pull through this though. We'll find Amelia's bones and put that spook to rest. Maddie will get some strength from that."

"How's it going out there?" I asked, trying to redirect my thoughts. A part of me desperately hoped that we'd uncover something... anything that would help Maddie.

Kat's face brightened a bit. "Actually, it's been going pretty good. I think Chris is making progress. I can barely see the top of his head when I'm standing next to the well. He must be about twelve feet down by now." She paused and rolled her eyes. "Normie tried to dig a few times last night to spell Chris, but honestly, he didn't get much done. You'd think someone so tall and lanky would have more muscle."

I couldn't help but offer a weak smile at Kat's teasing. It was comforting to hear her familiar banter.

"Have Norman and Chris had any rest? We're all running on fumes."

"Both of them took a nap earlier this morning," Kat informed me. "Slept in the van for a couple of hours. Chris seems hell-bent on finishing that dig today, or tonight at the latest. What about you? Have you managed to get any sleep?"

I hesitated before answering, glancing back at Maddie's delicate figure. The reality was, every time I shut my eyes to sleep, I dreaded what I might see when I woke. And after the terrifying vision I had just experienced, I was in no hurry to drift off again.

"Off and on," I admitted with a small shrug.

Kat noticed the flowers sitting on the table next to Maddie. Her eyes widened in shock at their wilted and drooping state, petals scattered around the vase like fallen tears.

"Holy crap, those were fresh just yesterday! Let me get rid of them for you."

She reached to grasp the vase, her fingers just beginning to touch the smooth glass as Maddie stirred, her eyelids fluttering open as if she'd been roused by an invisible hand.

"Leave them!" Maddie rasped, her voice sounding nothing like her own. It was deep, guttural, almost unnerving. Kat and I exchanged wide-eyed glances, both recognizing the chilling tone as Amelia's voice.

"Leave... them." Struggling to finish her words, Maddie

fell unconscious once more.

"Guess they stay here," I announced quietly, casting a wary glance at the wilting bouquet.

⇒⇒ ··•·· ⇐⇐

Chris's muscles burned with exhaustion. Darkness pressed in on him, unforgiving and relentless as his fingers scraped at the damp, cold earth. Dirt and mud clung to his body, his breath visible in the cold air. A sense of claustrophobia began to overwhelm him, causing his chest to tighten and ache.

"C'mon," he muttered, trying to silence the nagging voice in his head. "Let's get this over with... I know you're here... you have to be."

He studied the walls of the well, the rough stones arranged in a circle around him. The cramped space forced him to half-kneel as he dug, his back braced against the cool damp wall. It was evident that whoever filled in the well had done so hastily, the earth was a mix of loose dirt, rocks, and bits of wood. He was grateful that there wasn't any standing water, which would have made digging nearly impossible.

"Yo, Boss!" Norman called down, his voice echoing slightly. "Need a break?"

"Nah... I'm good."

Norman nodded and set his steaming cup of coffee down near the edge of the well, watching as Chris continued his almost frantic digging.

"I can smell the coffee, Norman," Chris called out with a smugness that made it clear he knew Norman was taking a break.

"Ah... yeah... a small cup." Norman quickly moved the mug away from the edge, fanning the air in hopes of dissipating the tempting aroma. "I'll make you one next time you're up."

A low rumble of thunder echoed through the valley, causing Chris to freeze mid-motion, the small shovel in his hand hovering over the bucket. He tilted his head back and squinted up at Norman, who looked equally startled.

"Did you hear that?" Norman called down, his voice tinged with surprise.

"Yeah, I heard it," Chris replied, gripping the shovel tighter. "How's the sky looking?"

"Clouds on the horizon... they're heading our way." Norman cast a nervous glance at the encroaching darkness. "I'd say we have a couple of hours, maybe more before the rain gets here."

Chris's heart sank. "Damn," he muttered under his breath. Time was running out. With a surge of adrenaline, he dug into the well floor, flinging spades of dirt into the pail. "Bucket!" he called out to Norman and watched as it slowly moved up the side wall, bits of dirt spilling as it traveled upwards. Chris shielded his eyes from the falling debris, his thoughts turning to the impending storm. Rain could make the well unstable, and if it filled with water... Chris shook his head. The thought of failure, the possibility that they might not find Amelia, weighed heavily on him. "Give me a break," he whispered to himself, as much a plea to the universe as it was to his own situation. The empty bucket found its way back to the bottom of the well.

"Have you changed out the hard drives for the cameras?" Chris called up, his voice echoing off the ancient stones.

"Uh, it's been a couple hours, but I can go ahead and switch to new drives if you want."

"Might as well," Chris said, pausing to catch his breath. "And while you're at it, reposition the lights and one of the cameras so we get better coverage down here."

"Will do," Norman replied, moving quickly to follow Chris's instructions.

Chris resumed digging, dirt clinging to his damp brow. He swore he could feel the atmosphere thicken as the storm approached, a ticking time bomb waiting to release its fury.

"Norman," he yelled, urgency coloring his tone. "Find a tarp or something to cover me, just in case."

"Copy!" Norman shouted back, his voice mixing with another distant rumble.

⋆»———◆———«⋆

It seemed the day had lasted an eternity. Light that once filled the windows was replaced by darkness. Fireflies began to appear outside, their tiny lights flickering in the distance. Every so often, a muffled rumble of thunder sounded, breaking the silence that hung heavy in the air.

I was alone with Maddie in her room. Kat left us hours ago, probably to give me time alone with Maddie.

I crouched beside the bed, my head lying on the mattress, arms draped across Maddie's frail body. I couldn't help but think about how terrible this day had been. Maddie had become more restless as the hours wore on, writhing around, mumbling incoherently. I could only offer her water, trying to coax her into taking even the smallest sip. When she refused, I dampened a cloth and gently wiped her brow, hoping to bring her some small measure of relief.

Another wave of restlessness seized her body. She twisted and turned, her limbs flailing wildly. It seemed as if she was trapped in a nightmare, fighting a monster I couldn't see.

"Please, God, help her." I prayed, my voice trembling. Maddie's spasms stopped, and she lay still once more.

The room grew cold, the chill seeping into my bones as I sat there, shivering beneath a blanket. Maddie's breath came in weak exhales, each one visible in the icy air. The temperature seemed to drop with each passing minute. I couldn't shake the feeling that something was about to happen, something beyond my understanding.

The room began to glow faintly, a green tint mixing with the warm glow from the lamp. My eyes landed on the bouquet of flowers that sat wilted and lifeless on the table, their once vibrant petals now limp, as if mourning their own demise. It seemed fitting, I thought bitterly, that as Maddie's life and beauty withered away, so too did the flowers.

The green glow intensified, and my eyes couldn't help but be drawn to the window. Fireflies had begun to land on the screen outside, casting their eerie luminescence into the room. I watched as the insects danced in unison, their tiny lights flickering like a morbid chorus, taunting me with their presence.

An airy rasp filled the room. "Sam... I'm here."

A flicker of movement caught my attention. I turned to see a small girl huddled in the corner, knees drawn to her face. Shadows clung to her like a shroud, obscuring her features, but there was no mistaking the fragile form of Amelia.

"No!" I called out, fear gripping me as I stared at the apparition. "Leave her alone!"

Amelia remained motionless, her face hidden. I noticed the dirt that stained her legs, and the small circle of wet mud on the floor around her bare feet. I wondered what horrors this lost soul had experienced.

"She doesn't deserve this... she shouldn't have to suffer like you," I yelled, my voice trembling with emotion.

Maddie's voice, thick with the guttural tone of Amelia's presence, cut through the oppressive silence that had settled over the room. "It's close..." she said, her words seeming to hang in the freezing air.

"What's close?" I asked, staring directly at Amelia.

"Everything."

A gurgling noise accompanied the words, a sound that made me think Maddie was choking. My eyes darted back to her, my hands trembling as I reached out to wipe the phlegm running from the corners of her mouth. I brushed the tangled, sweat-soaked bangs away from her brow, my fingers lingering for a moment on the feverish skin. After a few shallow breaths, Maddie's lips moved with the quiet, low tone of Amelia's voice.

"It'll all be over soon."

The cold air seemed to tighten its grip around me, squeezing the last remnants of hope from my chest. I clung to Maddie's fragile form, my fingers digging into the damp sheets beneath her. My mind raced with thoughts of all we had been through together, the love we had shared, and the unbreakable bond between us. Summoning a final surge of strength, I turned my gaze towards the small, huddled figure in the corner of the room. Amelia lifted her head, as if knowing I needed to speak directly to her.

"Will you take care of her?" I asked, my voice breaking.

Amelia nodded, her eyes never leaving mine. A glimmer of kindness flickered within their haunted depths, like a candle's flame struggling against a gust of wind. And then, as if responding to our unspoken agreement, the fireflies outside the window began to glow in unison.

In that instant, I knew the truth: these tiny, luminous creatures were waiting. They were guardians of the unknown, sent to guide Maddie into the next realm, to a place beyond the suffering and darkness that had consumed her life. The air in the room seemed to hum with anticipation, as if the very fabric of reality was beginning to unravel at the seams.

※

Kat leaned over the open hole in the ground, her eyes straining to pierce the darkness below. The tarp that covered the opening fluttered slightly, shaking the makeshift tent-like structure formed by a couple of poles tied to its edges. Chris's voice echoed from the well. "Bucket's full."

"Bucket's full," Kat repeated. She grasped the rough rope tightly, her hands already chafed from hours of labor, and pulled with all her remaining strength. Inch by inch, the heavy bucket laden with dirt emerged from the depths.

With a last heave, Kat guided the full pail out from under the tarp and carried it towards one of the many mounds of earth that had been forming over the past day. Norman was sprawled against a nearby pile, his arms extended outward as if crucified by exhaustion. Kat couldn't resist the opportunity for some levity. With a mischievous grin, she dumped the contents of the bucket onto Norman's legs, partially burying them beneath the dirt. Norman didn't move. He merely sighed in resignation.

"I'll have your sorry butt buried with a few more trips, Normie."

"I'd welcome that," he replied, his voice weak yet tinged with candor.

"Whiner," Kat teased before turning back towards the open hole, a hint of a smile playing on her lips.

She lowered the bucket and rope into the well, sensing, even at this distance, that something wasn't quite right. Chris sat on the damp floor, legs drawn up to his chest as he hid his face with his knees. He didn't move to retrieve the empty pail as it approached, allowing it to bump against his shoulder before coming to rest at his feet.

"You okay, Chris?"

"I think so," he replied without moving, his voice rough with exhaustion. Kat could see the fog of his breath form around his head.

"I'm burying Normie out here with the dirt... putting him out of his misery," Kat called down, hoping to provide a momentary distraction. "Want me to throw a few buckets over you?"

Chris couldn't help but laugh at the thought of Norman lying half-buried in the mounds of dirt. His snickers reverberated through the well, then quickly faded. A somber realization crept over him, a feeling that perhaps his work had been in vain. Another rumble of thunder rolled overhead, seeming to emphasize his sense of failure.

"I think we're done, Kat," he called up, lifting his head to peer up the long, narrow stone channel. He estimated that he must be at least thirty feet below the ragged entrance above. Kat's silhouette was rimmed with a pulsating green glow. Fireflies darted back and forth behind her, swarming with a curious intensity.

"Your call," Kat yelled down, an obvious sadness in her voice that only served to amplify the weight of his decision.

Chris took a deep breath, his mind racing. He could feel the oppressive darkness closing in around him, a tangible force that strangled his last remaining shreds of hope. Tears welled up in his eyes, more from exhaustion than sadness, but it was hard to separate the two as he realized that he had failed. Amelia wasn't in the well, and he was no closer to putting her spirit to rest than when he started. His thoughts turned to Sam and Maddie, and a knot formed in his stomach.

"Damn," Chris muttered, his voice barely a whisper. He clenched his fists, feeling the cold mud seep between his fingers. "What am I going to say to them?"

The weight of failure pressed down on him like the tons of earth above his head. His grip tightened on the small shovel, knuckles turning white. A primal scream tore from his throat as he thrust the spade into the muddy ground at his feet. "Goddammit!" he bellowed as he repeated the action, each plunge fueled by anger and frustration.

The last ounce of strength drained from his body with one final strike. A hollow thud and the sound of cracking wood echoed in the well. Chris froze, stunned. He drove the shovel deep into the ground again, and this time a stronger 'thud' of something solid reverberated in the silence around him. He tossed the shovel aside and began digging with his hands.

"There's something down here!" he cried out, clawing at the mud as if possessed.

"What is it?" Kat questioned, excitedly.

Slowly, Chris unearthed several planks of wood that laid at an angle against one wall. "These were used to cover the well" he thought, and a startling truth overwhelmed him… he'd reached the bottom.

Chris yanked one board away and tossed it to the side, then another. A small opening appeared between the boards. He peered into the darkness.

"Kat, drop that light down here… string it out and let it down more so I can see!"

"Normie's laying on it," Kat replied. She pulled at the electric cord, freeing it from Norman's pile of dirt without disturbing him. Slowly, she lowered the lamp down to Chris.

Light cascaded down the well as the lamp descended, casting shadowy fingers across the stone walls. Something glinted in the void, something shiny that would appear then fade as the shadows shifted.

"What the hell..." Chris muttered, his hands trembling slightly. The lamp finally reached him, and he grabbed hold of it, angling its beam to illuminate the void. Chris gasped, his breath escaping him in one last elated and fearful scream. "My God!" he yelled, unable to contain his shock. In the darkness, the sight of a skeletal hand emerged, its grasp firmly holding a golden locket.

"Amelia?" Chris mouthed as he stared at the partially mummified remains. Patches of black skin clung to exposed bone. He could make out the painted nails on fingers twisted and contorted like a broken branch, tightly intertwined around the golden necklace. Chris's breath caught in his throat, a creeping sense of dread filled him as reality sunk in. This wasn't the outcome he expected.

"What do you see?" Kat's excited voice cut through his thoughts.

"I'm not sure." Chris struggled to find the right words. The outstretched hand, with fingers curled like talons ready to strike, was that of a young woman.

"I've found human remains... but it's not Amelia."

"Not Amelia? You sure?" Kat's voice wavered as she processed the information. "If it's not Amelia then who the hell is it?"

I think it's Allison."

"You're shitting me!" Kat screamed, "Allison?"

"Allison."

The name escaped Chris's lips again. A combination of sadness and guilt weighed heavily on him as he came to terms with this new reality. He had uncovered a devastating secret, but it was a truth that marked the end of their search for Amelia.

A sudden blinding surge of green light filled the well, causing Chris to cover his eyes. Kat screamed and fled from the entrance as thousands of fireflies swarmed above, their presence like a living, pulsating cloud. They ventured down into the hollow column of stone, quickly reaching Chris at the bottom.

"What the... stop!" Chris shouted, raising his arms to shield his face. He swatted at the insects surrounding him, panic setting in as he crouched lower to escape the swarm. The light grew brighter, filling the well and temporarily robbing him of his sight. The buzz of the wings filled his ears, drowning out the pounding beat of his heart, but only for a moment. In an instant, the well fell silent and the green light vanished. Only the dim glow of the lamp remained to illuminate the area around him. Blinking away the spots that danced before his eyes, Chris glanced back into the void beneath the boards, adjusting the angle of the lamp for a better view.

His breath hitched – the skeletal hand was empty. The golden locket had disappeared. As if on cue, the sound of thunder rolled through the well, louder and more ominous than before. Chris's ears rang, and another sound started to build in intensity: gentle taps against the tarp above escalated until they became a deafening roar. It was now raining heavily.

"Shit," Chris muttered under his breath, his mind racing with fear and frustration. He stared at the empty skeletal hand, wondering what unseen force had taken the locket, and why. Was it Amelia? Or something darker, something malevolent?

"Chris!" Kat's voice echoed down the well, her tone laced with fear. "We gotta get you outta there! It's pouring!"

"Right!"

Chris forced himself to focus. He couldn't afford to stay in the well any longer, to take any more time to unravel this mystery. A new danger was becoming all too real. He struggled to his feet, his legs aching from the hours he had spent crouched. He could barely straighten them as he called up to Kat.

"Tie off the bucket rope to something that can hold my weight! I'll climb out!"

Kat disappeared and the rope tightened. It alternated between limp and taut as she was obviously tying the other end to secure it. Water began to roll down the sides of the stone well, at first a trickle, then in sheets that cascaded like a waterfall. Chris looked down. The hole had filled with water, once again hiding its secrets. The well was beginning to fill. Chris felt the water rise above his feet and onto his ankles. It was as if the well had come alive.

"Come on, Kat!" Chris muttered to himself, wiping water from his eyes as he glanced up into the darkness above. The rope tightened one last time, and he tested its strength against his weight. "Atta girl," he yelled out before slowly beginning his climb.

The water had risen alarmingly fast. It was inches from the lamp that was still burning brightly below him. If the water reached the light, Chris could be fried. His mind filled with horrifying images, his body convulsing in the electrified water, the skeletal hand reaching up to drag him under. Chris shook his head, trying to dispel the nightmarish thoughts.

"Kat... Kat the light!" Chris screamed, his voice echoing through the damp and chilling well. He gritted his teeth as he pulled harder on the rope, desperation seeping into his core. Pressing his back against the cold stones of the well's side, he lifted his feet and used the opposing wall to brace himself, inching upward with each strained pull.

The electrical cord stretched tight as it snagged on a board. With a sudden jerk, the lamp flew upward and crashed against the stone wall, shattering its fragile glass. The last flicker of light died in a rain of sparks that cascaded over Chris, their brief lives extinguished like desperate souls reaching out for salvation. The cord snaked its way up and over the edge of the well. Another brief flash of sparks filled the darkness as the broken lamp met water above.

Chris realized he hadn't been zapped, and he let out a deep sigh of relief. Darkness engulfed him once again, as he continued his climb. Every muscle in his body screamed in agony as they strained, tearing at the very fibers that held them together.

"Almost there," he whispered to himself, his breath ragged and uneven. Chris's mind became a battlefield, filled with thoughts of what he had seen in the void below: the skeletal hand of a woman clutching a golden locket, an enigma shrouded in mystery. The rope bit into his hands, but he refused to let go, knowing that if he did, he would plummet back into the watery abyss.

Norman had joined Kat at the well's edge. Seeing the water rising beneath Chris, he laid down and leaned over the side, stretching out both arms. "Grab my hands when you get close!"

"I'll help!" Kat yelled, her voice trembling slightly as she watched Chris struggle. Without waiting for a response, she clambered onto Norman's back, using her weight to anchor him to the ground.

"Come on... you got this!" Norman called out, his hands outstretched, willing his friend to reach him. Chris's fingers brushed against Norman's, and with a final surge of adrenaline-fueled strength, he managed to grasp hold.

"Got you!" Norman grunted, straining against the weight of Chris' waterlogged body. Kat's scream of joy pierced the tense air as she jumped up to grab Chris, pulling him away from the well. Her sudden movement caught Norman off guard, and he teetered on the edge, his arms flailing wildly. "Help!" Norman cried out, his voice cracking as he struggled to regain his balance. Kat's laughter mingled with his screams, creating a racket that only heightened the chaos of the moment.

Chris lay on his back, trembling with exhaustion, barely able to process the commotion around him. The rain had tapered off to a slow drizzle, then stopped. Kat leaned over him, making faces at Norman who was still complaining loudly.

"You did that on purpose!" Norman yelled, crawling backwards from the well's edge.

Kat playfully taunted him, arching her eyebrows in a suggestive manner. "Like I would ever let anything happen to you."

Chris noticed a strange green glow reflecting off the side of Kat's face. It pulsated like a heartbeat, growing brighter with each passing second. Intrigued, he propped himself up on his elbows, turning his head to search for the source of the light. "Guys, look," he whispered, his voice shaky but insistent.

Kat and Norman fell silent, their attention drawn to the same mesmerizing sight. In the distance, the farmhouse was enveloped by thousands upon thousands of fireflies, swirling and flying in intricate patterns. The window to Maddie's room appeared to be the epicenter of the phenomenon, with insects piling on top of one another, their lights pulsing in unison.

"Maddie?" Kat questioned.

"Maddie," Chris confirmed, his eyes locked on the stunning display.

Chapter Eighteen

Saying Goodbye

Life threw these moments at me, where I knew I was in the middle of something extraordinary, a brief experience where time itself decided to spill its secrets. The awareness that I was witnessing something special heightened my sense of gratitude and amplified the realization that life, with all its complexities, was an intricate tapestry of remarkable occurrences waiting to be acknowledged and appreciated. It was a sensation akin to standing on the precipice of something amazing, knowing that what unfolded wasn't just a fleeting event, but the final page of a book that I was fortunate to witness firsthand.

I sat there on Maddie's bed, her small body beside me barely stirring as her breaths grew labored and shallow. A loud crack of thunder reverberated through the room, shaking the walls, and rattling the windows of the old farmhouse. I turned to look at my precious Maddie, wondering how much longer we had together.

Outside, a peculiar, undulating green glow started to seep into the air, weaving its way through the window, and enveloping the room in an eerie luminescence. The wilted flowers beside the bed took on an otherworldly aura, their contours defined by an ethereal light that danced in unsettling shadows across the table. The atmosphere was charged, almost electric. I could feel it in my bones, something extraordinary was happening.

The glow intensified. My gaze shifted towards the corner of the room where Amelia had been sitting. She was no longer alone. Another specter, a young woman, had joined her, and Amelia had thrown her arms around her in a loving embrace. It was clear to me that Amelia was with her mom, Allison.

Outside, the rain began to pour, its intensity roaring against the windowpane, drowning out all other sounds except for the occasional rumble of thunder. A lump formed in my throat, and I found myself once again overcome by emotion. How could I still feel so much after everything I'd been through? After all the torment and heartache, knowing that my own child, Maddie, would soon be gone?

"Amelia...Allison," I whispered, my voice barely audible above the cacophony of the rain. Their ethereal forms shimmered like moonlight on water, their love for one another palpable even across the divide between worlds.

"Mama..." Amelia whispered, her voice filled with love and longing as she held onto Allison tightly. "I've missed you."

Allison knelt at Amelia's feet, her ethereal form shimmering like the reflection of stars on a still pond. I watched, transfixed, as they embraced each other with all the love that had been denied them for so many years. It was an embrace that could have lasted for an eternity if not for Allison's desire to provide Amelia with a gift – a gift she had been longing to share with her since that fateful night in the loft, when a desperate man's rage had torn them apart. The rain outside ceased abruptly, leaving behind a hush that wrapped around us like a gentle blanket.

"Amelia," Allison's voice resonated through the room, warm and loving as if spoken by an angel. "Do you remember that I wanted to give you a necklace when we were last together?"

Amelia nodded, and tears filled her eyes.

"You refused to wear it until I told you the truth."

From within the folds of her spectral gown, Allison produced a delicate locket, the golden surface glinting softly in the dim light.

My heart clenched in my throat, a surge of emotion flooding me as I grasped the profound meaning behind this seemingly ordinary object. To Allison, it embodied an unbreakable bond of love, a sentiment that transcended words. For Amelia, it held the weight of truth, unveiling the answer to a question that had echoed through her entire existence.

"Your father," Allison said gently, her eyes locked with Amelia's, "was Lawrence Laine."

Amelia's eyes brimmed with tears, which Allison tenderly wiped away before fastening the charm around her daughter's neck. As if drawn by the power of this moment, fireflies began to circle outside. They gathered on the window, their combined luminescence filling the space with an otherworldly radiance.

"Know this truth," Allison whispered, her eyes shimmering with boundless adoration. "From this very moment, we share no more secrets." Allison's ethereal fingers delicately traced the intricate carvings of the amulet now cradled around Amelia's neck. "This binds us for all eternity, and in its embrace, you'll forever sense the depth of my love."

The stairs creaked beneath the weight of hurried footsteps. Kat, Chris, and Norman had no idea what awaited them as they reached the top step. They froze in unison, eyes wide with wonder as they took in the sight before them: Allison and Amelia locked in a tearful embrace.

"Wh-what's happening?" Norman stammered, his hands shaking slightly as he clutched onto the railing for support.

"Shh," Kat whispered, her usual brashness giving way to quiet awe. She glanced at me, as if checking for my approval and making sure Maddie and I were okay. Chris, seasoned in investigating the paranormal and having encountered many things, stood frozen. This surpassed anything he had faced before.

As we watched, Amelia released her embrace from Allison, looking down at the locket that lay gently against her chest. Her gaze quickly darted to Maddie, lying motionless in the bed. She sensed something, and I felt it too. The air seemed to thicken as I held my breath. Time slowed, stretching each heartbeat into an eternity. And then, it happened—Maddie's chest rose and fell one final time. In that moment, I knew,this was the end.

"Maddie!" I screamed, my voice choked with grief.

"No... NO!" I flung myself across her, sobbing uncontrollably, holding on to her frail body as if I could somehow anchor her to this world even as she slipped away.

Kat crumpled to her knees, her grief pouring out in gut-wrenching wails. Her mascara-streaked cheeks were a testament to the raw anguish she felt at witnessing Maddie's final moments. Chris dipped his head in silent prayer for Maddie's soul, his lips moving quietly as he communed with a higher power. Norman, who had always been able to hide behind his bookish façade, was not immune to the pain that swirled around us like a tempest. He wiped tears from his eyes, trying to maintain some semblance of composure even as he mourned the loss of a life that had touched him so deeply.

Amelia seemed to understand our pain. She exchanged a knowing look with her mother, Allison, who nodded in understanding. With a grace that seemed otherworldly, Amelia glided across the room to the edge of the bed where I lay draped over Maddie's still form.

"Sam," Amelia said softly, her voice laced with sorrow, "I want you to have it."

I looked up, wiping my tears away as I watched Amelia. She removed the talisman from around her neck and held it out to me. The gold glinted in the dim light, the intricate design beckoning me to take it.

"Amelia...I can't," I hesitated, my eyes fixed on the necklace. "This belongs to you and your mother."

"Please," pleaded Amelia, her gentle pale blue eyes brimming with understanding. In that poignant moment, a profound connection unfolded through her genuine act of giving, lifting an unseen veil between us. It dawned on me: the precious offering she extended was more than a golden locket. It was a tangible promise of truth and everlasting love.

The sensation of Amelia's touch was like the gentlest brush of a cool breeze. "Thank you," I whispered, my fingers trembling as I accepted the necklace from Amelia's delicate, wraith-like hand. I felt the weight of the amulet in my palm, a tender reminder of the love that had transcended spiritual boundaries.

"Love never truly dies," Amelia said, her voice barely audible as she began to back away.

"Thank you," I whispered again, the enormity of the gesture leaving me in awe. Slowly, I turned back to my daughter, her body lying motionless on the bed. With trembling hands, I carefully clasped the locket around Maddie's neck, feeling the coolness of her lifeless skin. I recalled Allison's tender words and repeated them softly.

"Know this truth," I started, the words forming in my mind as if Allison herself were speaking them for me. "From this very moment, we share no more secrets." My fingers delicately traced the intricate carvings of the locket, just as Allison had done. "This binds us for all eternity, and in its embrace, you'll forever sense the depth of my love."

The room was suddenly filled with a blinding green light. It was the same light that had blinded Chris when he was in the well, and it seemed to pulse with an otherworldly energy. Maddie's skin began to shimmer with an ethereal radiance, as if she were merging with the light itself.

"Wh-what's happening?" Kat stammered, shielding her eyes from the intense glare.

"Stand back!" Norman warned, his voice shaking with a mix of awe and fear.

As the light enveloped Maddie completely, all of us watched, transfixed, unable to tear our gazes away despite the pain in our eyes. It was as if we were witnessing something truly divine, a moment that transcended the boundaries of our world. A clap of thunder echoed through the room, drowning out our collective gasps.

And then, just as suddenly as it had appeared, the light vanished.

The silence that settled over the room was deafening, a stark contrast to the chaos that had transpired moments before. I glanced around, searching for any sign of Allison and Amelia, but they were gone, vanished like a whisper on the wind. The fireflies that had once illuminated the window had departed, leaving behind an empty, almost eerie darkness.

"Guys, look at this!" Kat's voice broke through the quiet, her tone tinged with astonishment. We all turned our attention to the nightstand beside Maddie's bed, where a once-wilted bouquet of flowers now stood tall and vibrant, their petals awash in dazzling colors that seemed to defy the dim light of the room.

"Unbelievable," Chris murmured, shaking his head in amazement. Norman simply stared, unable to speak.

"Mama?" The sound of Maddie's voice, weak but unmistakably alive, pierced the silence that had settled over the room. I lifted my head, scarcely daring to believe what I was hearing.

There she was, my precious child, her cheeks flushed with color and her eyes bright with life. A radiant smile spread across her face as she reached for me, the gold locket around her neck sparkling in the dim light. "Mama, I missed you."

Tears streamed down my face as I grasped her outstretched hand, marveling at the warmth of her skin. Relief surged through me like a tidal wave, and I pulled Maddie into a tight embrace, unable to hold back the tears that flowed freely down my face. Kat rushed over, wrapping her arms around both of us, her own sobs mingling with mine in a symphony of joy and gratitude.

Norman, his usual stoic facade crumbling under the weight of emotion, laid his head on Chris's shoulder. Chris, taken aback by the unexpected gesture, managed only a half-hearted protest. "Really, Norman?"

"Shut up, Chris," Norman muttered, his voice thick with emotion. "I have feelings too, you know."

No one paid any mind to his complaint. Our focus was on the little girl lying in the bed, her body once again filled with the vibrant energy of life. The questions of how and why would surely come later, but for now, we simply reveled in the joy of this unexpected gift.

Chapter Nineteen

Fireflies

It was a warm summer day, the kind that wraps you in its golden embrace and makes you feel like anything is possible. Maddie, my little miracle, was running through the field by the farmhouse, her laughter ringing like bells in the air. She danced, twirling with arms outstretched as she gathered flowers.

"Chris, do you see her?" I asked, my voice thick with emotion. "She's so full of life!"

Chris wrapped his arms around me from behind, pulling me close. "She's playing hard... makin' up for lost time I guess."

Maddie's once pale face was now flush with color. She'd gained weight, and I swear she had grown an inch in just the last few months.

"I wanna catch this butterfly!" Maddie declared, chasing after the delicate creature as it fluttered away from her outstretched fingers. Her voice, filled with joy and wonder, brought tears to my eyes.

"Don't hurt it," I called out, my voice thick with emotion.

Shortly after Amelia's spirit was put to rest, Chris joined

us for a trip back to 'the city' to visit Maddie's doctors, a visit we feared could bring another round of devastating news. The tests lasted several days, and I could sense something had changed. Smiles replaced the usual averted glances as, one by one, the physicians read us the results. They confirmed what I already knew: no trace of the once fatal disease could be found. To me, the explanation for the miracle was simple. Love had healed Maddie.

"Everything's changed so much," I murmured, leaning into Chris. "It's like everything has just exploded."

Chris sighed softly as he lovingly pressed his lips against the back of my head. "Yeah, it's been pretty crazy since your articles about Amelia and Allison were published. I've had so many requests for interviews and speaking engagements I've lost count... same as you."

"Does it ever feel surreal to you?" I asked, rubbing my hands over Chris's arms, firmly wrapped around my waist.

"Every day," he replied, his voice tinged with wonder. "I guess fame goes with the territory though, right? I mean, me being such an amazing paranormal investigator and all." Chris chuckled as I spun around to challenge his conceit.

"Just kidding, love, I've turned down all the requests. It's your story that matters, you and Maddie, and honestly, I still need time to process everything we experienced."

"Testing, one, two..." echoed across the open field, interrupting my impending challenge to Chris's ego. Norman was testing the PA system set up for the evening's tour.

"Testing... testing... one, two..."

"Is that really necessary?" I asked, "There's only going to

be a handful of people here tonight, I'd rather it be a bit more intimate."

"I'll talk to him."

Chris unwrapped himself from our embrace and walked across the field to speak with 'Normie'.

I couldn't help but smile at Norman's dedication. In the past few months, he had taken on the self-appointed responsibility of answering the many inquiries from potential clients and fans. I recalled my latest visit to the Leesburg office, seeing his desk piled high with boxes and bags of mail.

"Sam, you should read this request we got," he'd told me excitedly during my last visit. "Apparently, there's a ghost haunting a bowling alley, tormented by being two pins short of a perfect game. The poor guy rolled a 7-10 split in the last frame and had a heart attack when he saw it... croaked right there on the spot. Now his spirits there every night - trying to roll his perfect game."

"I don't imagine that's good for business," I responded, smiling at the mental image.

"Probably not," Norman exclaimed and quickly grabbed another intricately decorated letter. He blushed, recognizing his name as the intended recipient - another personal fan letter from a female admirer.

I glanced over at Kat, who was sitting nearby casually flipping through a magazine and pretending to not pay attention. She retained her edgy personality, but there was a new softness about her that hadn't been there before. Her makeup was lighter, and her clothes less provocative. She seemed more at peace with herself. Still, she never missed an opportunity to taunt Norman, and his red face hadn't gone unnoticed.

"Aw, Normie, look at you! The paranormal heartthrob of Leesburg!" she teased, sensing that his red glow and smile was due to another letter from a female fan. Norman rolled his eyes, but I could tell he secretly loved the attention.

"Not seeing any letters here for you at the moment." He smirked as he slid a couple of envelopes beneath a tall pile, letters probably addressed to Kat.

My daydream was interrupted by the echo of a slight commotion, and reality returned. Norman's amplified voice was complaining vigorously as Chris tried to coax the microphone from his hand.

"It's not going to be like Karaoke... well... unless you want it to be."

The sun dipped low in the sky, casting the field in a golden hue as the tour bus rolled to a stop nearby. I could see Kat leading the invited guests off the bus, her arms raised above her head with glow sticks in hand. She hawked them for a small fee to anyone interested in having a piece of their glowing light. Kat was still very much Kat.

"Welcome, everyone," she called out, her voice carrying across the field. "Find your seats and get ready for an evening you won't forget."

Our Ghost Tour team had assembled today to conduct a special tour, one not open to the public. These were not our usual tour attendees: thrill-seekers and ghost enthusiasts eager for a scare. Instead, they were individuals who had experienced losses of their own and sought solace in the understanding that a connection between the spiritual world and the physical world existed. They had read of our paranormal encounters with Amelia, of Maddie's friendship with the spirit, and they hoped to find some comfort in hearing the tale firsthand.

As our guests settled onto the wooden benches, I felt a sense of peace wash over me. Chris took my hand and together we walked to the front of the crowd. Behind us, a field of grass undulated in the gentle breeze, like waves on a tranquil sea. An occasional firefly appeared over the grass, adding a touch of magic to the scene.

"Thank you all for being here tonight," I began, after introducing myself to the crowd. My voice trembled slightly, but I took a deep breath and continued. "In this very place, we encountered a lost spirit, a little girl named Amelia." As I spoke, I saw Amelia's face in my mind's eye, her big, bright eyes gazing at me with warmth and understanding. I looked over at Maddie, who offered a small, encouraging smile. "Amelia and my daughter Maddie became friends," I said softly, my heart swelling with gratitude for the connection they had forged. "Together, they guided us on a journey of discovery and healing that would change all of our lives forever."

The crowd listened silently, their expressions a mixture of curiosity and wonder. I detailed our journey to uncover the truth behind Amelia's disappearance and her connection to Allison, her mother.

"Through mysterious signs and whispers from beyond, Amelia led us to the truth about her mother, Allison's, fate. She showed us where her mother's bones lay hidden within an old well on this property, and with them, a golden locket that held the key to their reunion."

Tears glistened in the eyes of many in our audience as I shared the story. They were silent, captivated by each word as it left my lips. Chris, Kat, and Norman joined me at the front to share their experiences, and finally, it was left to me to bring the presentation to a close.

"When I placed the locket around Maddie's neck," I whispered, emotion thickening my voice, "the love that bound Amelia and Allison together transcended the barriers between our world and the next, healing my daughter's illness and setting their spirits free."

I paused for a moment, taking in the sea of faces before me. "Love is light..." I whispered, feeling the weight of those words settling over the crowd like a warm blanket. "... and light is eternal."

The sun had vanished below the horizon, leaving the field bathed in twilight. As I finished speaking, the first fireflies of the evening began to emerge, their tiny lights flickering like stars amidst the tall grass.

The purr of an engine broke the silence, announcing the arrival of a sleek, dark SUV limousine. Norman shrugged and Kat scanned her clipboard for any names that may have been unaccounted for, but neither could offer any explanation for this unexpected arrival. Intrigued, Chris and I walked towards the car, now parked next to the tour bus. The driver stepped out and opened the back door, revealing an elderly woman seated inside, her sharp eyes fixed on us with an intensity that, at first, startled me. A second woman, whom I guessed to be in her mid 70s, emerged from the opposite side and walked around to assist the older woman from the car. She was strikingly beautiful, even in her advanced age, and her attire spoke of wealth and refinement.

Nodding at the driver, the younger woman helped the elder to her feet, and we approached them with cautious curiosity. "I'm Samantha, and this is Chris," I said, offering a warm smile. "We've just finished our presentation, but we'd be happy to answer any questions you may have."

The elderly woman's voice was strong and resonant as she replied, "I'm pleased to finally meet you both." Chris and I exchanged puzzled looks as she held out her hand. "I'm Alba Weston, Director Emeritus of the Laine Foundation."

I was speechless, as if the weight of our shared history had temporarily stolen my voice. "Alba... ma'am," I managed to say finally, "I'm honored that you came to visit us today." Chris nodded in agreement, his expression mirroring my own mixture of awe and surprise.

"Thank you," she replied, her voice steady. Turning to the woman beside her, she introduced her companion. "This is a fellow board member and my assistant, Angel... Angel Laine."

Angel had long gray hair and piercing blue eyes that seemed to contain an ocean of memories. She gave us a warm, genuine smile.

"Angel, it's a pleasure to meet you," Chris said graciously, extending his hand. Angel nodded and smiled warmly.

"Thank you both for your offer to answer our questions, and I can assure you there are many... but we've come here to share some things with you as well."

Alba turned her gaze back to me, her eyes filled with concern. "Samantha, I've read in your article that your daughter is now well... I'm so happy to have learned that."

"She's our little miracle." Sam dropped her gaze for a moment, feeling a bit intimidated by Alba, wondering if she believed in Maddie's healing.

Alba gently took my hand in hers and moved closer to me. "When I agreed to let you and Maddie stay at the farmhouse, I felt like there was a reason for it, some kind of spiritual destiny, perhaps. Her voice softened almost to a whisper. "Your visit has brought about healing for both of us."

Angel steadied Alba as she turned and moved closer to Chris. "There is much more to the story than you know," she began, her tone solemn. "I was in constant contact with Allison over the years, and when her letters and calls went unanswered, I grew increasingly alarmed." She paused for a moment, collecting her thoughts. "I contacted George Benningly, who admitted that Lawrence had become somewhat unhinged... the drinking and all. He feared that Lawrence had tried to contact Allison."

Alba glanced at Angel who stood by her side stoically. Angel patted her arm, as if to encourage her to continue. "I contacted the local authorities, instigating the search for Allison and Amelia. You can imagine how upset I was to learn that both had seemingly vanished. I knew Lawrence was involved, but I chose to keep quiet... the man could be quite intimidating as you can imagine." Alba's gaze turned to Angel, standing by her side. "It was complicated... and there were others to consider."

Angel's expression didn't change at the mention of her father's name. It seemed she had long ago dealt with the emotions that surrounded her father's involvement in Allison and Amelia's disappearance.

"Alba," I said, my voice trembling, "your strength and courage have made all the difference in this story, not just for Amelia and Allison but for us as well. You did all you could."

"Thank you, Samantha," she replied with a gentle smile. "My only wish is that I could have done more to help them."

"Your actions made it possible for us to find the truth," Chris reassured her, his eyes shining with sincerity. "And now, their spirits are finally resting in peace."

"Forgive me for interrupting, but I have something to share as well." Angel stepped forward a little, her arm still supporting Alba. She looked at Chris with the same piercing blue eyes that Amelia must have inherited. "I met Amelia shortly before she went missing... I was riding my horse and came upon her when she was playing, here in this field. Her voice softened as the memories filled her. "I gave her a ribbon I had won, and she loved it so much... I promised to give her all my ribbons when I won. Angel paused briefly and looked towards the horizon. "I felt such a connection to her... and I was so upset when I learned she had disappeared." Angel's eyes welled up and she glanced at Alba, who took her turn at offering encouragement.

"After the show, I rode to the farmhouse and left a blue ribbon on the back steps, hoping that one day she would come home and find it."

"Did you ever see her again?" Chris asked softly.

"No," Angel shook her head. "But over the years, I continued to leave ribbons for her. It was my way of keeping a connection alive, even if it was only in my heart."

As she spoke, I could feel the power of her love for Amelia, and it touched me deeply. Chris told Angel about the many ribbons we had found in the cellar, hanging from the rafters like silent witnesses to a promise kept. She stared at him, stunned, and tears welled up in her eyes.

"Amelia got my ribbons," she whispered, visibly moved. "She knew... I kept my promise."

Maddie tugged on my hand. She had joined us without me noticing, and I pulled her towards the group. Her eyes were bright and curious as she looked at Alba and Angel. Chris introduced her, and as Maddie shyly greeted them, I felt warmth radiating from their smiles.

"Your time at the farmhouse has been special, hasn't it?" Alba asked me.

"Yes," I replied, thinking of all the love, and healing we had experienced here. "But we'll be returning to New York soon."

"Stay," Alba said simply. "The Laine Foundation has granted you ownership of this property. It's yours, now and forever."

I blinked back tears, overwhelmed by her generosity. "Thank you," I whispered, my voice choked with emotion.

"Maybe there's another reason you'd like to stay?" Alba

glanced knowingly at Chris, a subtle comment that hinted at the growing connection between us.

Thousands of fireflies flickered into existence, their tiny lights dancing like stars scattered across the grassy field. The guests spoke in hushed whispers as they took in the breathtaking sight, their eyes filled with wonder and disbelief.

"Is it true, Maddie?" Alba asked, bending down to address her directly. "Did you really see Amelia's spirit?"

Maddie nodded solemnly, her small hand clutching mine tightly. "Yes," she whispered, eyes shining with conviction. "She's there now." She pointed towards the field, where countless fireflies swirled like a living constellation.

Alba followed Maddie's gaze, and I could see her eyes widen as she spotted two figures standing in the distance. It was Allison and Amelia. A knowing smile spread across her face as she turned to Angel who supported her frail frame. "Help me walk into the field," she requested. "I want to see them up close."

"Let me take you," Maddie offered, extending her free hand towards Alba. Together, they began to walk into the field, the fireflies' gentle glow illuminating their path.

Tears welled up in my eyes as I watched them go, and I felt Chris's strong hand encircle mine. "Do you want to go too?" he asked, his voice tender and understanding.

I nodded, unable to speak through the emotion that threatened to choke me. Kat, who had been silently watching, asked if she could join us, and we welcomed her into our small procession as we ventured further into the field.

One by one, other guests began to follow, stepping hesitantly into the pasture as if pulled by an invisible force. Some murmured the names of their lost loved ones, their eyes searching the flickering lights for a sign of their presence.

Fireflies circled around us, their delicate wings brushing against our skin like whispers, welcoming us into their world of light and love. The sight was nothing short of magical, and as we approached Allison and Amelia, I was reminded of the words I had shared earlier, words that Amelia herself had spoken:

"Love is light, and light is eternal."

In that moment, as we stood together beneath the twinkling night sky, I knew that the love we held for one another would never fade. It would continue to shine on, a beacon of hope and comfort amidst life's darkest moments. For love, like the light of the fireflies that surrounded us, is eternal... boundless, transcendent, and everlasting.

Congratulations on finishing the book! If you enjoyed the journey and connected with the story and characters, please consider leaving a review. Your feedback helps others discover the book. Also, a portion of each sale supports a charity for terminally ill children and their families. Thank you for being a part of this meaningful cause!

About the Author

K. D. Phillips, the imaginative mind behind the captivating novel "A Darkness Between the Stars," has now released her eagerly awaited second work, "Fireflies."

With an enduring love for storytelling, KD's journey as an author is a testament to her lifelong passion for the written word.

Born in the heart of Alabama and raised in the scenic landscapes of Georgia, KD's upbringing planted the seeds of a profound appreciation for the potency of words. From an early age, she delved into countless literary realms, fostering her creativity and fueling her vivid imagination.

"Fireflies" is not just a novel; it is a tapestry woven with threads of KD's own experiences. For several years, she resided in a farmhouse on Old Waterford Road outside of Leesburg, Virginia. The vivid descriptions in the book mirror the very walls of the residence she once called home. KD's daughter, Kirsten, encountered paranormal phenomena, such as glimpses of a mysterious woman reflected in her bedroom mirror. These encounters prompted KD to seek insights from a paranormal investigator who led local ghost tours. The authenticity of these experiences served as the wellspring of inspiration for the mesmerizing narrative of "Fireflies."

Now nestled in the sun-soaked landscapes of Florida, KD continues to draw inspiration from the vibrant world around her. With her husband by her side, she nurtures her creativity, weaving stories that transcend boundaries and kindle the flames of imagination. Join KD on her literary adventures as she invites readers to explore the enchanting realms she crafts with words, proving that the best stories are often born from the rich tapestry of lived experiences.

Made in the USA
Columbia, SC
02 April 2024